Celebrating the Christian Year

Alan Griffiths is a priest of the Roman Catholic Diocese of Portsmouth. He studied Liturgy at the Pontifical Liturgical Academy of Sant' Anselmo in Rome and taught liturgical studies at Saint John's Seminary, Wonersh, from 1977 to 1983. He was a member of the panel that produced *Opening Prayers, Scripture-related Collects for Years A, B and C from the Sacramentary* (Canterbury Press, 1999) and has translated the Ambrosian Eucharistic Prefaces, published as *We Give You Thanks and Praise* (Canterbury Press, 1999). He has worked as a drafter and editor of texts for a National Proper collection commissioned by the Roman Catholic Bishops Conference of England and Wales. He works currently as a liturgical consultant active in the field of Church building and renovation.

Also available from the Canterbury Press
Celebrating the Christian Year
Volume 1: Ordinary Time

Forthcoming
Celebrating the Christian Year
Volume 3: Advent, Christmas and Epiphany

www.scm-canterburypress.co.uk

Celebrating the Christian Year

Prayers and Resources for Sundays, Holy
Days and Festivals – Years A, B and C
Volume II: Lent, Holy Week and Easter

Compiled by Alan Griffiths

CANTERBURY
PRESS
Norwich

© in this compilation Alan Griffiths 2005

First published in 2005 by the Canterbury Press Norwich
(a publishing imprint of Hymns Ancient & Modern Limited,
a registered charity)
St Mary's Works, St Mary's Plain,
Norwich, Norfolk, NR3 3BH

www.scm-canterburypress.co.uk

British Library Cataloguing in Publication data

A catalogue record for this book is available
from the British Library

ISBN 1-85311-602-5

Typeset by Regent Typesetting
Printed and bound by
Biddles Ltd, www.biddles.co.uk

CONTENTS

INTRODUCTION

This is the second volume of *Celebrating the Christian Year*, a liturgical resources collection for the Sundays and festivals of the Church's Year.

The first volume covered the Sundays and feasts, as well as other events, of the Sundays and weeks from Pentecost to All Saints' Day, All Saints' to Advent, and Epiphany to the Presentation of the Lord, or Candlemas. This second volume covers the season of Lent, the Three Days of Easter and Eastertime concluding with Pentecost.

Like the first volume, this collection follows the course of the Lectionary as set out in *Common Worship*. I hope this will render it usable not only in Anglican congregations, but also in other church communities that use the *Revised Common Lectionary*, which is very close to that of *Common Worship*. The Roman Catholic Lectionary too is similar, indeed historically it is the inspiration for the other two. So I hope that Roman Catholic communities also might make use of some of these texts. Roman Catholics will find here much that is familiar to them from the Roman Missal, though in fresh translations.

This is a resource collection and not a complete service book. I have not included the outline or standard texts for services, or (with one exception) texts that are repeatedly used, such as those for the Intercession. These differ between traditions, denominations and churches. I hope people will make use of the texts contained here in whatever way they find appropriate.

As in the first volume, I have tried to maintain a liturgical style that echoes the English styles currently used in most of the major denominations. As in all liturgical books, some of the prayers will require preparation on the part of those who speak them. Everyone who exercises the great privilege of presiding at common prayer knows that one can't just walk into church and read texts unseen. I have tried to make them as uncomplicated as I can, however.

In particular, I have been trying to develop a fresh approach to the way God is named and addressed. The terms 'God' and 'Lord' and their associated adjectives 'almighty', 'eternal', and so on, are the forms of address most commonly encountered in worship books. However, I think there is a need to name God in other, more diverse ways.

The materials for this are close to hand. The Bible and the tradition of the Church offer us a rich diversity of address when naming God. It is a well-tried principle to look for our prayer language in the Scriptures. The psalms in particular yield language that is vital and direct, portraying images of God that speak to people far more significantly and inclusively than do many of the ways of address we have become accustomed to. I have tried to draw on this richness.

Some introductory remarks on the nature of the liturgical seasons are appropriate here, as these form the basis on which I have chosen material for this book.

Easter

In the Christian Year, the Festival of Easter, with its fifty-day sequel leading up to Pentecost, has the primary place. Easter comprises the period that begins on the evening of Maundy Thursday and ends on the evening of Easter Sunday. It should be considered and celebrated as one single three-day event, rather than as the sequence of individual commemorations we have been accustomed to in the past.

Easter is the greatest feast of the calendar, and occupies the position in the sacred year that Sunday occupies in the sacred week: it is both the beginning and the 'end'. Easter is not simply the remembrance of Christ's resurrection. It is the feast of his whole 'Passover' from death to life.

Easter is the Christian Passover. That is its name in ancient and many modern languages: *Pascha* in Greek and Latin, *Paques* in

French, *Pasqua* in Italian and so on. It might even happen that in time, and with the increasing secularization of British society, English-speaking Christians might decide to drop 'Easter' in favour of 'Pascha' as many English-speaking Orthodox Christians do nowadays. 'Easter' is a word of pagan origin. 'Passover' is a rich and allusive term, a title inherited from Judaism (and maybe older than that) and invested with new meaning by the Christian tradition from the very beginning.

For Christian believers, Passover means the crucified and living Christ (cf. 1 Corinthians 5:7). Christ has 'passed over' from this world to the Father (cf. John 14:18–21). Easter represents their personal 'Passover' with Christ, enacted in the Sacrament of Baptism (cf. Romans 6:1–6). In recent years, there has been a growing interest in adult baptism and initiation, as people become Christians in adult life. Also, society is less inclined than previously to baptize babies as a sort of 'naming' or 'dedication' ceremony. Indeed, within some churches there is a growing sense that such a convention represents a misuse of this primary sacrament.

This growing interest in adult Christian initiation has led to the recovery of the ancient link between Easter and Baptism. Adults are now likely to be baptized, confirmed and come to the Eucharist for the first time during the Easter Vigil, at the conclusion of a period of training, discernment and immersion in the life of Christian community. In the texts of this volume, therefore, baptismal themes occur frequently.

As the Christian 'Passover', the feast of liberation from the power of death, Easter is also eschatological, a feast of the things to come, the remembrance of the eternal Passover into life, which awaits us all on the final great 'Day of the Lord'. Easter propels us forwards; the resurrection is the event that moves us beyond ourselves into the future 'rising that promises the glory of all flesh' that Christ has in store for us. Easter is an enactment of the present reality of Christ – alive for ever as the One slain – and of our reality as those called to be 'in Christ', that is, those called to a corporate life that gives form in this present age to the Body of Christ, animated by the Holy Spirit, who is the agent of the things to come.

The Easter season lasts fifty days. This is a sacred counting of time, seven weeks of seven days plus one, the 'last and greatest day', the day of Pentecost. Each day of Easter is a festival. The Sundays are not described any longer as 'Sundays after Easter' but as 'Sundays *of* Easter' – an important distinction. Easter calls forth the best we have – our greatest rejoicing as believers, best quality bread and wine, the best vestments and music.

The Easter Season includes the Festival of Christ's Ascension, forty days after Easter. Ascension initiates a change of tone in Eastertide, as it begins to look towards Pentecost. This week between Ascension and Pentecost may be seen as a sort of 'octave' (the seven days following the really great festivals of the Church) of Pentecost celebrated before the day itself. Pentecost has no octave as such, since it is the last day of Easter. The High Priestly Prayer of Jesus is an appropriate Gospel reading for the time between Ascension and Pentecost. This prayer of Christ is interpreted by the worship tradition of Christianity as a prayer for the coming of the Holy Spirit on the Church, a theme already present in the *Book of Common Prayer* with the Collect for the Sunday after Ascension, and further elaborated in *Common Worship* by the first extended Preface for this time.

Lent

To prepare for the Three Great Days of Easter, there is the season of Lent. In the past, Lent has been understood as a forty days period imitating Christ's sojourn in the desert, following the theme of the First Sunday's liturgy, a time for 'giving up' things. However, the primary meaning of Lent has come to be a period of preparation for Easter.

Among Christians, this preparation for Easter, the 'feast of feasts', will take the form of a renewal of their common faith, expressed in different ways for different groups of Christian people.

As mentioned already, Easter is increasingly the time for bringing new Christians into communion with their fellow believers.

Introduction

For those adults preparing for Baptism at the great Vigil service of Easter, Lent will be a time of looking forward to the fullness of the practice of Christian prayer, worship and living according to the gospel. They will be readying themselves to experience the sacraments of Christian Initiation: Baptism, Confirmation and Communion for the first time.

For others, the observance of Lent can be a time for rediscovering the meaning of sacraments that they received as babies or young people. Lent can also be a time of penitence, or retreat, or simply a time to tackle once again the basics of faith.

In all these ways, Lent offers everyone a time to re-engage with an authentic Christian spirituality, one whose main lines of thought, prayer and action are symbolically enacted in the worship of the Church.

Lent, then, is far more than a memory of Jesus' temptation in the wilderness, or just a time to 'give things up'. Among images that the Lenten liturgy employs in the Gospel and other readings on Lenten Sundays are the great paradigms of faith in Jesus: the calling of Abraham, the Journey of God's people through the desert towards the Promised Land, the stories from Saint John's Gospel of the Samaritan woman, the Man Born Blind and the raising of Lazarus. Also there are the images of God's love and acceptance of repentant sinners such as the Parable of the Prodigal Son.

The Christian gospel announces forgiveness and reconciliation with God. This is not only enacted liturgically, but also through the three disciplines of Christian living. The Lent liturgy speaks often about them: prayer, fasting and charitable works. These things, as many ancient Christian teachers maintained, are the normal way by which Christians both seek forgiveness for sins and express thanksgiving for God's freely given grace in Jesus Christ.

Lent lasts approximately six weeks, from Ash Wednesday until Maundy Thursday. It is marked by restraint. Christians are called to abstinence – self-denial in food and drink – and the tone of the liturgy is subdued. The acclamation 'Alleluia' is not heard throughout the season. Elaborate music and the use of instruments are traditionally minimized; the colour of vestments and hangings is muted: blue, violet or plain cloth, to maintain the tone of starkness and simplicity.

Lent itself changes tone as Easter approaches, with the fifth Sunday and the week after being more focussed on the Passion of Christ as Holy Week approaches. Finally, Holy Week, also known as 'The Great Week' in some Christian traditions, begins with the triumphal entry of the Messiah into the Holy City and moves towards the climax, the three Holy Days of Easter itself.

The Contents of this Volume

Prayers and prefaces are proposed in this book for all the Sundays and major feasts that occur during Lent and Easter.

- For each occasion, a **Scripture-related opening prayer**, or collect based on the Scripture readings (one for each of the years A, B and C of the Sunday cycle) is given.

- An alternative collect or **opening prayer** is also provided. The Scripture-related opening prayer and the second opening prayer might be chosen as alternatives to the collect proposed in *Common Worship,* or used at other times in worship as appropriate.

- Gospel **Acclamations** to be used with the refrain 'Alleluia' (or another refrain in Lent when 'Alleluia' is not sung), are also included.

- A third collect is then given. This prayer, usually built around the theme of the Church, is intended for use at the conclusion of the **Intercession.**

- The **Prayer over the Gifts** is a prayer that should be used after the preparation of the Lord's Table and the 'taking' of the gifts of bread and wine.

- A **Eucharistic Preface** is given for each Sunday and feast.

- A **Prayer after Communion** concludes this series of texts.

For the weekdays of Lent and Easter, a collection of collects, prayers over the gifts, prefaces and prayers for use after Communion is included. Where there is a daily Eucharist these prayers will be appropriate. They might also be used in the daily Office or other prayer.

Sources and Translation

Many of the prayers in this book derive from the Latin Missals of the Roman and Milanese ('Ambrosian') Church, which together form the most extensive collection of liturgical prayers in current use, as well as being the source of most of the collects in the *Book of Common Prayer* tradition and a real 'school of prayer'. Here, and wherever prayers are translated from Latin sources, the translations are my own. In translating I have tried to give the sense of the original while not slavishly following the syntax. Latin syntax can sometimes be reproduced in English. More often, attempts to reproduce it yield an English that sounds distinctly off-key.

With some prayers, particularly with the prayers over the gifts used at the Preparation of the Table, I have adapted rather than translated. The language of 'offering' the bread and wine is found frequently in the Latin originals of these prayers. This causes difficulties for many Anglicans and indeed such language can be problematic for Roman Catholic liturgical theology too. So for this moment in the service I have tried to produce prayers that look to the Eucharistic Thanksgiving or Communion, or that speak of the fellowship and peace to be found at the Lord's Table.

For the Sundays of Lent, the prefaces vary according to the year of the Lectionary cycle, in order to take up the theme of the Gospel for the Sunday. The Sunday and weekday prefaces are mostly drawn from the Ambrosian Missal mentioned above, the ancient Eucharistic Liturgy of the Milan Diocese. This Missal contains a magnificent collection of over three hundred Preface texts from a liturgical book revised, like the Roman Missal, after the Second Vatican Council. The translations of the prefaces are based on those in my book *We Give You Thanks And Praise – The Ambrosian Eucharistic Prefaces* (Canterbury Press 1999).

A Prayer after Communion is suggested for each occasion. The themes of these are not simply Communion-oriented but look forward to the implementation of worship in mission, as people leave the church to 'love and serve the Lord'.

Outside the Eucharist or main service, I have also included suggestions for other services. The Way of the Cross is a devotional service popular in many churches, particularly during Lent. A special Holy Week service based on the medieval office of Tenebrae is also included. I have also outlined a service for Good Friday that uses the Passion according to Saint John as the basis for a processional liturgy. For some congregations this might suggest ways of being creative and providing a workable alternative to the rather static traditional rites for that day. I have also given texts for evening prayer of Saturday, a service that might form either a prelude to Evening Prayer or else the basis for a vigil service of Sunday, as suggested in *Common Worship*.

There is some music included in this collection. In Volume One a small amount of simple chant was included. Here the quantity is greater. This is to make the singing particularly of responsorial material – a mode unfamiliar to many Anglicans and Free Church people – more easily accessible. This music is pretty basic and makes no claim to sophistication. However, I can testify that it works in congregations with only minimal resources, without organ or choir, and that it is easy to learn.

The Conclusion of Collects

Collects usually end with an acknowledgement that prayer is made to the Father through Jesus Christ. The traditional short ending is '(We make this prayer/we ask this) through Jesus Christ our Lord.' For a more 'solemn' ending, often employed with the opening Collect, the Trinitarian relationships are invoked in something like this form:

Through Jesus Christ your Son,
who is one with you and the Holy Spirit,
now and for ever.

This echoes, with less elaboration, the traditional ending found in *Common Worship* collects.

Such endings may be used with most of the collects in this book. I have tried to vary the endings, partly to allow for those who prefer to avoid terms such as 'Lord' and 'reigns', partly to allow for variety. Those who prefer to use the more traditional endings will find that they are usable with most of the collects given in the body of the text.

The Beginning and Ending of the Prefaces

Traditionally, the first line of the preface echoes the congregational response: 'It is right to give thanks and praise' – 'It is truly right . . .'.

I have usually kept to this traditional opening for the prefaces in this book:

It is truly right and just, our duty and our salvation,
always and everywhere to give you thanks,
Lord, holy Father, almighty and eternal God,
(through Jesus Christ our Lord).

There are variants on these openings and endings in the prefaces suggested in this volume. The principal variant is that used during Eastertide, where there is a specific paschal reference in both the opening and ending of the preface:

It is truly right and just,
our duty and our salvation,
to praise you, Lord God, in every season,
but most of all in these most holy days
when Christ, our Passover, is sacrificed.
. . .

Introduction

And so, in the joy of Passover,
earth and heaven resound with gladness.
The angels and the powers of all creation
sing the ageless hymn of your glory: Holy . . .

The variant preface opening most often used in this book resembles the traditional 'echo' opening by echoing an earlier line of the dialogue between president and congregation: 'Lift up your hearts', and begins something like this:

We lift up our hearts to you,
God eternal, true and faithful;
to you we offer thanks and praise
through Jesus Christ your Son.

Preface openings are usually interchangeable, so if this form is preferred, it can be used with most of the prefaces in this book.

The preface ending also varies. The traditional ending names the various ranks of heavenly beings, angels, archangels, thrones, dominions, powers and so on. In older liturgical books, these endings were sometimes very elaborate and reflected the interest in the orders and degrees of angelic beings:

And so, with angels and archangels,
thrones and dominions,
and with all the powers of heaven,
we glorify your holy name
in this, their ageless hymn of praise:

However, there are other, shorter forms, such as

And so, with angels and saints,
we glorify your holy name:

Again, these preface endings are usually interchangeable. The dynamic of the liturgy demands, however, that the congregation is cued to enter with 'Holy, Holy . . .'.

Introduction

The Scripture-related opening prayers are, by and large, longer than most of the other prayers in this book. In the first volume of this collection, these prayers were laid out as single paragraphs. Further reflection prompted me to change the layout of these texts by dividing them into paragraphs on the model of the layout of the Eucharistic Prefaces, which are texts of comparable length. I hope this will make them easier to prepare and speak.

Lastly, I have included a form of the Eucharistic Prayer in this volume. I am aware that the liturgical regulations of most mainstream Church traditions will preclude the use of this text. Nevertheless, I decided to include it more as a specimen of what one could say, and as a prayer that was attempting in various ways to engage creatively with the (sometimes) contentious issues of Eucharistic consecration and sacrifice. This prayer began life some twenty years ago with the International Commission for English in the Liturgy (ICEL) who were at that time engaged in a revision programme for the Roman Catholic Missal. My original version has undergone several complete overhauls since that time and this seems to be its final form.

I have gained much, both in learning and in pleasure, from the compilation of *Celebrating the Christian Year*. I hope that this volume, like its predecessor, will offer both a source for planners and leaders of worship, and something also that people might profitably use for spiritual/devotional reading.

Alan Griffiths
1 May 2004

PART ONE

PROPER TEXTS FOR
THE SUNDAYS OF LENT

Lent extends over six Sundays, the last of which is Palm Sunday. In this section prayer texts are suggested for all the Sundays of Lent together with details of ceremonies that are associated with those Sundays.

The First Sunday of Lent

One of the ways of identifying this opening Sunday of Lent is to begin the Eucharist with a procession of the whole congregation and the ministers, singing a litany. The Litany given in Common Worship *may be used. The following alternative litany text names the saints of the Church as part of the fellowship of Lenten observance.*

The Saints' names given in this form of litany are suggestions. Others should be added (the Patron of the church or parish, local figures, etc.) where necessary and in the appropriate place in the list. Other petitions might also be inserted in the second section.

Cantor: Lord, have mercy	*All repeat*
C: Christ, have mercy	*All repeat*
C: Lord, have mercy	*All repeat*

Saint Mary, Mother of God:	R/. Bless the Lord! *or*
	R/. Pray for us!

Proper texts

Saint Michael:
All angels of God:
Saint John the Baptist:
Saint Peter and Saint Paul:
All the apostles:
Saint Stephen:
All Martyrs of Christ:
Saint Athanasius:
Saint Basil:
Saint Augustine:
Saint Martin:
Saint Benedict:
All holy men and women:

Lord, come to our aid: R/. Lord, save your people.
From every evil:
From all that divides us:
From everlasting death:
By your Incarnation:
By your death and resurrection:
By your ascension:
By the gift of the Holy Spirit:

Remember us, O Lord: R/. Lord, hear our prayer.
Forgive us our failings:
Reconcile our enmities:
Grant us your peace:
Bless this time of Lent:
Bless us in prayer:
Bless us in self-denial:
Bless us in works of love:
Bless all those preparing for Baptism:
Jesus, Son of the living God:

The procession may end with the Scripture-related opening prayer or alternative opening prayer. The Ministry of the Word follows as usual.

Scripture-related opening prayers

Year A
God, our Saviour,
by the free gift of your grace in Christ
you have brought new life
to the children of Adam and Eve.

Recall for us the story of your mercy
and renew our faith in your salvation;
teach us, during this Lent,
to live by your word,
trust in your protection
and worship you alone.

We ask this through Jesus Christ,
who is one with you and the Holy Spirit,
now and for ever.

Year B
God of creation,
you stretched forth your bow in the clouds
as a promise of your goodwill for creation,
and in the outstretched arms of Christ crucified
you desire to embrace all men and women.

Let us, who are baptized into Christ's death,
be clothed in the likeness of his resurrection,
so that your Church may truly become
the ark of safety for the whole human family.

We ask this through Jesus Christ,
who is one with you and the Holy Spirit,
now and for ever.

Year C
God, our stronghold,
you brought your people out of slavery
and you desire freedom for all men and women.

Let your word be close to your people,
so that both from the lips and from the heart
we may speak of your wonderful deeds,
and let the first-fruits of our liberation
be fulfilled in a rich harvest
of peace for humankind.

We ask this through Jesus Christ,
who is one with you and the Holy Spirit,
now and for ever.

Opening prayer

Grant to us, almighty God,
that through the observance of Lent
we may understand more deeply
the riches hidden in Christ,
and apply their wisdom
in the conduct of our lives.
We make this prayer through Jesus Christ our Lord.

Acclamations

Year A: Matthew 4:4
V/. Christ our Saviour, glory to you!
R/. Christ our Saviour, glory to you!
V/. No one lives by bread alone,
but by every word of God.
R/. Christ our Saviour, glory to you!

Year B: Psalm 25:9
V/. All the paths of the Lord are mercy and truth,
to those who keep his covenant and his testimonies.

Year C: Psalm 91:11
V/. He shall give his angels charge over you,
to keep you in all your ways.

Intercession

God, our guide,
you have made known to us the way of life.
Guide your Church along this path,
and bring us home to you,
for with you is our lasting peace.
We ask this through Jesus Christ our Lord.

Prayer over the Gifts

Creator God,
we pray you to fashion our lives
in the likeness of Christ,
whose table we share
and of whose life we partake.
We ask this through Christ our Lord.

Eucharistic Preface

It is truly right and just, our duty and our salvation,
always and everywhere to give you thanks,
Lord, holy Father, almighty and eternal God,
through Jesus Christ your Son.

By fasting forty days
Christ gave us the pattern
for this time of self-denial.
By resisting the temptation of the enemy
he taught us to reject the leaven of malice and wickedness
that we might celebrate his Passover in sincerity and truth
until we reach its fulfilment
in the promised land of your kingdom.

And so, with angels and archangels
and with all the hosts of heaven,
we glorify your holy name
in this, their ageless hymn of praise: Holy . . .

Prayer after Communion

God of our pilgrimage,
sustain us, that we may always walk
in the strength of this living bread.
We ask this through Christ, our Lord.

The Second Sunday of Lent

Scripture-related opening prayers

Year A
God, our glory,
you opened Abraham's eyes
to the wonderful vision of his destiny,
and by water and the Holy Spirit
you have made us able to perceive your kingdom.

Deepen this faith you have bestowed,
and open the hearts of many
to that love which has so loved the world.

We ask this in the name of Jesus,
who is one with you and the Holy Spirit,
now and for ever.

Year B
God, our glory,
you gave a son to Abraham and Sarah
and foretold among their descendants
the coming of your Christ,
the Son of Man who was to be rejected.

Let us not weaken in faith
before the hostility of the world,
but give us courage
to take up the cross and follow Jesus,
who is one with you and the Holy Spirit,
now and for ever.

Year C
In darkness and mystery, O God,
you called Abraham to trust your promise
and you gave him the faith to follow that call.

Bless our keeping of Lent,
so that by your grace we may fulfil
our baptismal calling to serve you
by prayer, self-denial and the works of love,
trusting that Christ will transform our lowly body
in the glory of the eternal Easter;

for he is one with you and the Holy Spirit,
now and for ever.

Opening prayer

God, our Father,
you desire that everyone should be saved
and that no one should be lost.
Change our hearts
as we strive to keep this time of Lent,
that our lives may draw others to you,
and our weaknesses not deter them.
We ask this through Christ our Lord.

Acclamations

Year A: John 3:14
V/. As Moses lifted up the serpent in the wilderness,
so must the Son of Man be lifted up,
that whoever believes in him may have eternal life.

Year B: Mark 8:34
V/. Jesus said: 'If any want to become my followers,
let them deny themselves and take up their cross
and follow me.'

Year C: Psalm 27:16
V/. I believe that I shall see the goodness of the Lord
in the land of the living.

Intercession

God, our hope,
we cry out for your saving help,
for without you we can do nothing.
Grant that your people
may know what is right, do what is just
and follow your purpose in all things.
We ask this through Jesus Christ our Lord.

Prayer over the Gifts

Lord God,
teach us the wisdom of your table,
and in our sharing of your gifts
draw us closer to you
in love of one another.
We ask this through Jesus Christ our Lord.

Eucharistic Preface

We lift up our hearts to you,
God of holiness and glory;
to you we offer thanks and praise,
through Jesus Christ your Son.

You bid your faithful people cleanse their hearts
and prepare joyfully for the Easter feast.
You call us to prayer, self-denial and the works of love,
so that by celebrating the mysteries
through which we are born again,
your people may be brought
into the fullness of Christ, the risen Lord.

And so, with angels and saints,
we glorify your holy name: Holy . . .

Prayer after Communion

We receive these holy gifts
and give thanks to you, our God,
because you allow us, while dwelling on earth,
to share already in the blessings of heaven.
We make this prayer through Christ our Lord.

The Third Sunday of Lent

Scripture-related opening prayers

Year A
God, fountain of holiness,
you cause the living waters of grace
to flow from the rock that is Christ.

Pour into our hearts
the Holy Spirit of your love,
that we may find new faith in you,
and let the conduct of our lives
announce the great things
that you have done for us.

We ask this through Jesus Christ,
who is one with you and the Holy Spirit,
now and for ever.

Year B
Holy God,
you display the depth of your wisdom
in the cross of Christ.

Let that wisdom fashion us anew
as a community of faith,

of obedience to your commandments
and of longing for your justice.
Draw us into the depths of your mystery,
and in the body of the risen Christ
give to us that holy place
where we may serve you in peace.

We ask this in the name of Jesus,
who is one with you and the Holy Spirit,
now and for ever.

Year C
Faithful God,
you desire us to turn away
from things that do not satisfy
and find our fulfilment in you.

Have patience with us,
tend and nurture our faith
and make us bear the fruit of true conversion
to the praise of your grace and mercy.

We ask this through Jesus Christ,
who is one with you and the Holy Spirit,
now and for ever.

Opening prayer

God of compassion, source of all goodness,
you have shown us that prayer,
self-denial and works of love
are the healing for our wounded humanity.
Look upon us now
as we acknowledge our weakness,
and when our conscience weighs us down,
raise us again in your abiding mercy.
We ask this through Jesus Christ our Lord.

Acclamations

Year A: John 4:14
V/. 'The water that I will give,' says the Lord,
'will become a spring, welling up to eternal life.'

Year B: John 2:21
V/. The Lord spoke of the temple of his body,
and after he was raised from the dead,
his disciples remembered his words.

Year C: Matthew 4:17
V/. 'Repent,' says the Lord,
'For the kingdom of heaven is near.'

Intercession

God, ever present to your people,
make us persevere in our quest for holiness,
and while we seek to serve you in this present age,
set our hearts on your eternal glory.
We ask this through Christ our Lord.

Prayer over the Gifts

Gracious God,
as we come to your table,
reconcile us to one another,
that our communion in Christ
may truly give you praise.
We ask this through Christ our Lord.

Eucharistic Prefaces

In Year A, when the Gospel of the Woman of Samaria is read
Father, all-powerful and eternal God,
it is truly right to give you thanks

and a joyful thing to honour you with praise,
through Jesus Christ our Lord.

When he asked the Samaritan woman
for water to drink,
Christ had already bestowed on her the gift of faith.
Now in his compassion he thirsted for that faith,
and kindled in her heart the fire of your love.

And so, with angels and archangels
and with all the host of heaven,
we glorify your holy name
in this, their ageless hymn of praise: Holy . . .

Year B
Father, all-powerful and eternal God,
it is truly right to give you thanks
and a joyful thing to honour you with praise,
through Jesus Christ our Lord.

By the hand of Moses your servant,
you gave to your people the ancient Law,
written on tablets of stone;
and now, by the gift of the Spirit,
you have prepared a new covenant,
written upon the heart,
so that men and women
may become your adopted children in Christ,
calling on you as their God and Father.

And so, with angels and all saints,
we glorify your holy name: Holy . . .

Year C
God of mercy and compassion,
it is good to give you thanks and praise,
because you continue to call us
to share the fullness of life.

Though we are sinners, you promise forgiveness,
and through the incarnation of your Son
you have bound us to yourself
in a new and unbreakable bond.
You give to us this Lenten season
as a time to draw breath for our journey to you,
to open our hearts to your Spirit
and respond to the needs of our neighbour.

And so, with angels and all saints
we glorify your holy name: Holy . . .

Prayer after Communion

In this sacrament, O God,
we receive the pledge
of things yet hidden in heaven
and are fed in our earthly sojourn
with food and drink from on high.
Let this gift work within us
so that we may bear the fruit
which will endure to eternal life.
We ask this through Christ our Lord.

The Fourth Sunday of Lent

Scripture-related opening prayers

Year A
God, whose face we long to see,
you have looked upon us in love,
and with the anointing of your Spirit
have opened our eyes to the insight of faith.

Let us not be afraid to acknowledge before the world
that Christ is the world's true light,

and bestir us to seek the fruits of the light
in everything that is good and right and true.

We ask this in the name of Jesus,
who is one with you and the Holy Spirit,
now and for ever.

Year B
God of steadfast love,
you have created us anew in Jesus Christ
for the doing of those good works
which you have prepared for us.

Set our hearts and minds on the One
who was lifted up for this world's healing,
and as we remember your goodness,
let us also live in your praise.

We ask this through Jesus Christ,
who is one with you and the Holy Spirit
now and for ever.

Year C
Compassionate God,
you run to embrace the penitent sinner,
and spread a feast to welcome home the lost.

Grant that we, being found and restored by grace,
may welcome our brothers and sisters
who long to find the security of your family,
and as we thank you for your forgiveness,
make us also a people who forgive.

We ask this through Jesus Christ,
who is one with you and the Holy Spirit,
now and for ever.

Opening prayer

God, our provider,
you created humankind in your likeness,
and sustain us in this present age
with the blessings of the age to come.
Make your people rich in spiritual gifts,
so that we, who by nature are creatures of this earth,
may be reborn as children and citizens of heaven.
We make this prayer through Christ our Lord.

Acclamations

Year A: John 9:5
V/. Jesus said: 'As long as I am in the world,
I am the light of the world.'

Year B: John 3:16
V/. God so loved the world
that he gave his only Son.

Year C: Luke 15:24
V/. This son of mine was dead and is alive again;
he was lost and is found.

Intercession

Gracious God,
you give us what we do not deserve
and you bless us with gifts beyond our imagining.
As you have so richly graced us,
so make us work untiringly for your kingdom.
We ask this through Christ our Lord.

to reveal the mystery of your Church,
your people brought to birth in baptism
and nourished with Christ's body and blood.

And so, with angels and all saints,
we glorify your holy name: Holy . . .

Year C
We lift up our hearts to you,
God of mercy and compassion;
to you we offer thanks and praise,
through Jesus Christ your Son.

Your boundless glory is shown in this:
that by your power as God most high,
you came to the rescue of our mortal nature.
Moreover, from that very mortality
you drew forth a healing remedy
as your eternal Word took on our human state
and made us partakers of your divinity.

And so, with angels and saints,
we glorify your holy name: Holy . . .

Prayer after Communion

God of light,
whose radiance illuminates all,
fill us with the splendour of your grace
that we may set our minds on things
that are fitting and pleasing to your glory.
We ask this through Christ our Lord.

Mothering Sunday

The prayers for Mothering Sunday may be used instead of those for the Fourth Sunday of Lent.

Scripture-related opening prayer

Years ABC
God of steadfast love,
you cradle us at birth,
embrace us at our life's end
and welcome us into your eternal dwelling.

Let such a tenderness move us
to love you in return
and draw others into the circle of your care.

We ask this through Jesus Christ,
who is one with you and the Holy Spirit,
now and for ever.

Opening prayer

God of creation,
in your gracious order,
family life has its firm foundation.
Listen in mercy to the prayers of your people
and teach us to imitate your motherly love
in our care for one another.
We ask this through Christ our Lord.

Acclamation

Years ABC: 2 Corinthians 1:3
Blessed be the God of all consolation,
who consoles us in all our afflictions.

Intercession

Be moved, O God,
by our weakness and fragility
and come to the help of the human family
with strength and support in all its need.
We ask this through Christ our Lord.

Prayer over the Gifts

Lord, you spread this table for us;
we pray that here you will feed your family
and strengthen them in fellowship
as the members of Christ.
We ask this through Christ our Lord.

Eucharistic Preface

It is truly right,
our joy and our salvation,
to give you thanks and praise,
most gracious God, our help and our saviour.

You gather your people
as a mother gathers her children;
and by Christ's anguish and labour on the cross
you have brought us forth as your sons and daughters.
Your goodness turns sorrow into joy,
your gentleness confounds our fear,
and at the last, your loving arms enfold us
into the joy of our eternal home.

And so, with angels and saints,
we glorify your holy name: Holy . . .

Prayer after Communion

With your holy gifts to feed us,
send us out, O God,
to show your care and love
for all your children.
We ask this through Christ our Lord.

The Fifth Sunday of Lent – Passion Sunday

Scripture-related opening prayers

Year A
Out of death, O God, you summon life:
dry bones to stand up among the living,
Lazarus to come forth from the tomb.

Breathe your Spirit into us,
unbind us and set us free:
for your glory is the human being fully alive
and our life, the sight of your glory.

We ask this through Jesus Christ,
who is one with you and the Holy Spirit,
now and for ever.

Year B
From one single grain, O God,
buried in the earth
and springing up triumphant on the third day,
you have grown a rich harvest.

In this Lenten springtime,
let the word of your truth
be sown deep in our heart,
to bear abundant fruit
in lives that glorify your name.

We ask this through Jesus Christ,
who is one with you and the Holy Spirit,
now and for ever.

Year C
God, before whom we bow in adoration,
make our prayer fragrant
as precious perfume before you.
Let our praise be proven true
by the practice of hope and faith.
Set our sights on the destiny that lies ahead,
and our hearts on Christ, our goal and prize.

We ask this in his name,
who is one with you and the Holy Spirit, now and for ever.

Opening prayer

God, our strength,
fortify your people
to walk in the way of your love,
that love which Christ so fully showed
in giving himself up to death
for the life of the world.
We ask this in his name,
who is alive, now and for ever.

Acclamations

Year A: John 11:25
V/. 'I am the resurrection and the life', says the Lord.
'Those who believe in me, even though they die, will live.'

Year B: John 12:24
V/. Unless a grain of wheat falls into the earth and dies,
it remains a single grain.
But if it dies, it bears much fruit.

Year C: Psalm 126:6
V/. Those who sow in tears
shall reap with songs of joy.

Intercession

Loving God,
bless those who put their trust in you,
and as you have planted in us
the desire to seek your face,
so at last reveal to us
the vision of your glory.
We ask this through Jesus Christ our Lord.

Prayer over the Gifts

God, our teacher in faith,
welcome us as we approach your table,
and by the sacrifice of praise
unite us in the body of Christ,
who is alive, now and for ever.

Eucharistic Prefaces

For Year A, when the Gospel of Lazarus is read
It is truly right and just, our joy and our salvation,
always and everywhere to give you thanks,
Lord, holy Father, almighty and eternal God,
through Jesus Christ our Lord.

As one who shared our mortality,
Jesus wept for Lazarus, his friend
and as the eternal God,
he raised Lazarus from the tomb.
In compassion for humankind,
Christ has led us, by the sacraments of faith,
into new and eternal life.

Through Christ, the angels
and all the hosts of heaven
praise and adore your glory;
let our voices join with theirs
in their unceasing hymn of praise: Holy . . .

Years B and C
One of these two prefaces is appropriate
It is truly right,
our joy and our salvation,
to give you thanks, all-holy God,
through Jesus Christ our Lord.

Through the saving passion of your Son
the whole world is called to acknowledge
how great you are, how worthy to be praised.
The power of the cross
reveals your judgement on this world,
and the kingship of Christ the Crucified.

And so, with angels and archangels,
and with all the powers of heaven,
we glorify your holy name,
in this, their ageless hymn of praise: Holy . . .

or:

It is truly right,
our joy and our salvation,
to give you thanks, all-holy God,
through Jesus Christ our Lord.

By the human nature which he assumed,
Christ gathers us all into his body;
humbled, he raises us up,
handed over to death, he sets us free;
his suffering redeems us,
his cross and passion saves us,
his flesh is our food, his blood, our cleansing.

And so, with angels and archangels,
and with all the powers of heaven,
we glorify your holy name,
in this, their ageless hymn of praise: Holy . . .

Prayer after Communion

Almighty God,
let us be counted among the members of Christ,
in whose body and blood we have communion.
We ask this through Jesus Christ our Lord.

Palm Sunday

Palm Sunday has a double focus. Ancient liturgies on this day commemorated either the Triumphal Entry of Christ into Jerusalem or his Passion and death. Later tradition combined these themes. The two forms of service offered here will allow either focus to predominate. Elements of both may be combined so that the procession in honour of Christ may precede the Mass of the Passion with the Passion Gospel.

First Form: Procession of Palms and Eucharist of Christ the King

On the Sunday before Palm Sunday, as a reminder to the people to prepare for the most significant week of the Christian Year, it is appropriate to make palm leaves available to the congregation, so that they may take some of them home, weave them together and decorate them with flowers and other greenery for Palm Sunday.

It is worth remembering that imported palm leaves and crosses are a relatively recent introduction to Christian practice. Traditionally, branches of box or other aromatic shrubs have been used. Many churchyards will have such shrubs growing to hand.

For the full procession, the congregation gathers in a place apart from the church. If a full procession is not possible, the rites take place at the church door with a representative body of clergy and congregation who process to the altar from there.

As the people and clergy gather, suitable songs may be sung. This Anthem is traditional:

Hosanna to the Son of David!
Blessed is the One who comes in the name of the Lord!
Hosanna in the highest!

The president greets the people:

V/. The Lord be with you.
R/. And also with you.

Dear friends in Christ,
our Lenten work is drawing to a close.
Today we gather
to honour the One who comes in God's name
and who will come again to set us free.
On this day Christ entered his holy City
where he was to suffer, die and rise again.
As we remember his coming
in humble triumph, riding on a donkey,
let us remember also his future advent
upon the clouds of heaven
to do justice for the living and the dead
and to unite us, his members,
in joy and glory with himself.

The congregation is invited to hold their palms up high.

The president says this prayer:

Bless us, O God,
as we acclaim the coming of Christ, your Son;

bless our gathering and open our hearts to that great day
when Christ will gather us to himself
in the new and heavenly Jerusalem.
For he is alive, now and for ever.

or:

Lord, we ask you to bless these branches.
In triumph today Christ comes among us.
May Christ lead us on our way
through his passion and death,
to his victory and eternal kingdom,
where he is alive, for ever and ever.

*The president may sprinkle the congregation with holy water,
if this is used, and may also incense them. Then another of the
ministers says:*

Let us make our way in peace,
following our Saviour
to the celebration of his holy mysteries.

*The procession then begins. During it, suitable hymns may be
sung.*

*The procession concludes at the chancel or sanctuary step, where
the president recites the Collect or opening prayer of the Day.*

Scripture-related opening prayer

Years ABC
Christ, our hope,
to you we come with hymns of praise,
echoing those who hailed you
as Messiah and king.

Make us honour you always
by doing the works of love and justice

your Spirit inspires in us,
so that when you come in glory
you may recognize us as those
who truly belong to you:
for you are the living One, now and for ever.

Opening prayer

Grant to us, we pray, almighty God,
the forgiveness of our sins by your mercy,
so that we may worthily prepare the way
for Christ as he approaches,
and through good works done by your grace
may obtain the palm of victory.
We ask this through Jesus Christ our Lord.

*For this service, and for all three years of the Lectionary Cycle,
the Old Testament Reading is Zechariah 9:9–10*

The Psalm is Psalm 72:1–14

The New Testament Reading is Romans 15:7–13

Acclamations

Year A: Matthew 21:5
V/. Tell the Daughter of Zion,
'Look, your King is coming to you.'

Gospel Reading: Matthew 21:1–11

Year B: John 12:13a
V/. Hosanna! Blessed is he who comes
in the name of the Lord!

Gospel Reading: either Mark 11:1–11 or John 12:12–26

Year C: Luke 19:38
V/. Blessed is the king,
who comes in the name of the Lord.

Gospel Reading: Luke 19:28–40

Intercession

Faithful God,
today your Son enters his city
to inaugurate the coming of his hour.
Let us share the blessing
you bestow on the poor in spirit,
that we may truly welcome him
as the Saviour of all.
We ask this through Christ our Lord.

Prayer over the Gifts

God, our joy,
let the praises we sing
and the communion we share at your table
give you glory.
We ask this through Christ our Lord.

Eucharistic Preface

It is truly right and just, our joy and our salvation,
always and everywhere to praise you,
God most holy, compassionate and good.

You sent your Son, Jesus, the Christ,
into this world for us and for our salvation,
so that by his humility
and acceptance of our mortal suffering,
he might call us back to fellowship with you.
As he entered Jerusalem to fulfil the scriptures,

the crowd welcomed him with faith and acclamation,
spreading their garments with olive branches in his way.

Now therefore, as the children sang his praises,
we also will lift up our hearts and voices
in tribute and joyful praise: Holy . . .

Prayer after Communion

Gracious God,
you nourish us in this present age
with food and drink from on high.
Through this holy feast,
make us partakers in the eternal glory of Christ,
who is Lord for ever and ever.

Second Form: Eucharist of the Lord's Passion

If this service is to begin with the blessing and procession of
palms, then, after the blessing prayer and before the procession
one of the Gospels indicated above (pp. 27–8) should be read.

The procession concludes with one of the Opening Prayers given
below.

Scripture-related opening prayer

Years ABC
To the weary and despairing, O God,
you send your word of deliverance
in Jesus, your servant and your Son.

As we begin this holiest of weeks,
draw us close to Christ
and let his mind be in us,
that in his obedience we may find
the strength to pursue your purpose
of new life and freedom for all.

We ask this through Jesus Christ,
who is one with you and the Holy Spirit,
now and for ever.

Opening prayer

Almighty and eternal God,
in the passion of Christ
you have brought us back
to fellowship with yourself.
Safeguard this work of your mercy,
and through our celebration
of the Easter mystery,
grant that we may live in faithfulness to your will.
We ask this through Christ our Lord.

Anthem before the Passion: Philippians 2:1–11

Christ was humbler yet,
even to accepting death, death on the cross.
But God has raised him on high
and given him the name
which is above every name.

The Passion of our Lord Jesus Christ

The Passion narratives of Matthew, Mark and Luke that are read on Palm Sunday may be proclaimed in a number of ways.

They may be divided up into parts, with one part for a narrator, another for Christ and a third (or more) for other voices. If the Passion is to be chanted, and particularly if there is a choir to render the crowd parts, this is an effective and moving form of proclamation. It should be noted that competent chanting takes no longer than competent reading.

A dramatized recitation is also suitable for a spoken Passion reading. The readers should include a 'chorus' to speak or chant the crowd parts. All the readers need to be well rehearsed and used to working together as a team. A version of such an arrangement is given in *Lent, Holy Week and Easter* (Church House Publishing, 1986, pp. 142–75). It is also possible to divide the Passion into sections (as opposed to dramatic roles) for several readers. This makes for a more equitable division. A good version of this is *The Passion of Our Lord Jesus Christ* (Liturgy Training Publications of Chicago, 1999).

The option exists, of course, for a solo reading, as is usual with the Gospel.

Another method of presenting the Passion is to adapt the convention common in post-Reformation Lutheran circles and elaborated by J. S. Bach. This is to divide the text, whether spoken or sung, into sections and insert appropriate hymns or other music. Many well-known passion hymns were used in the Bach passions, and may be so employed still. Taizé responses might also be employed, or instrumental music if that is possible. It would be appropriate also to have short silent pauses during the reading.

The notes that follow offer suggestions for the presentation of the Passion. These are appropriate both for the traditional (spoken) dramatic presentation or a reading divided among several readers. The basic division for the Synoptic Passions is similar, but of course they may be divided into longer sections than those suggested here.

The Passion according to Matthew (Matthew 26:14—27:66)

Three readers are required for this. It is recommended that the President not be one of them. They should stand where they may best be heard and seen. If possible, the congregation should stand for the Passion. The first reader introduces the Passion with the words:

Reader: The Passion of our Lord Jesus Christ according to Matthew.

Pauses are made during the reading of the Passion, during which everyone should be seated and a silence kept. Responses, songs or hymns may be sung or music played.

First Part: Matthew 26:14–34, Judas' betrayal, the Supper, the walk to the Mount of Olives

Suggested music: Taizé response 'Stay with me' (Bleibet hier) or 'Stay with us, O Lord Jesus Christ', or 'Though one with God, yet not by might' (paraphrase of Philippians 2:6–11) by John Bell and Graham Maule (which may be sung to the tune 'Ye banks and braes'), from *Love From Below*, or 'No weight of gold or silver (*Hymns For Today's Church* 138)

Second Part: Matthew 26:36–75, Jesus' prayer, the arrest, the trial before the Sanhedrin, Peter's denial

Suggested music as above, or the Iona response 'Jesus Christ, Son of God' (from John L. Bell, *Come, All You People*), or 'Drop, drop slow tears' (*New English Hymnal* 82)

Third Part: Matthew 27:1–31, Pilate, the soldiers mock Jesus

'O sacred head' (*New English Hymnal* 90, *Hymns for Today's Church* 139), 'See Christ was wounded for our sake' (paraphrase of Isaiah 53 in *Hymns for Today's Church* 137), Song of the Suffering Servant by Alan Rees OSB (paraphrase of 1 Peter 2:24 etc., in *Songs for the Church's Year*)

Fourth Part: Matthew 27:32–54, the Crucifixion and death of Jesus

Many of the above choices may be used, as well as: Taizé response 'Crucem tuam', Taizé response 'All you who pass this way', 'My song is love unknown' (*New English Hymnal* 86)

Fifth Part: Matthew 27:55–66, the Burial of Jesus

It might be appropriate to end the Passion with the hymn 'Praise to the Holiest in the height' (*New English Hymnal* 439).

The Passion according to Mark (Mark 14:1 — 15:47)

The reader will begin by announcing: The Passion of our Lord Jesus Christ according to Mark.

The Passion according to Mark is the shortest of the Passions. It may be divided up in a similar way to that of Matthew. Music choices will be the same as those set out above.

First Part: Mark 14:1–25, the Supper and the walk to the Mount of Olives
Second Part: Mark 14:26–51, the prayer of Jesus and his arrest
Third Part: Mark 14:52–72, the trial of Jesus, Peter's denial
Fourth Part: Mark 15:1–15, Jesus before Pilate
Fifth Part: Mark 15:16–24, Jesus mocked by the soldiers
Sixth Part: Mark 15:25–41, Jesus' Crucifixion and death
Seventh Part: Mark 15:42–47, the Burial of Jesus

The Passion according to Luke (Luke 22:14 — 23:56)

The reader will announce: The Passion of our Lord Jesus Christ according to Luke.

The Passion according to Luke may be divided up as follows.

First Part: Luke 22:14–38, the Supper, Jesus' charge to Peter
Second Part: Luke 22:39–62, Jesus arrested, Peter's denial
Third Part: Luke 22:63 — 23:25, trial before the High Priest, Pilate and Herod
Fourth Part: Luke 23:26–49, the Crucifixion and death of Jesus
Fifth Part: Luke 23:50–56, Jesus is buried

Music selections will be similar to those suggested for the Passion according to Saint Matthew. In addition, the Taizé response 'Jesus, remember me' is appropriate after the fourth part.

Intercession

Eternal God,
you have brought salvation to the human race
by the death of Christ, your Son.

Grant, we pray,
that this faithful celebration of his passion
may bear abundant fruit in the joy of Easter.
We ask this through Christ our Lord.

Prayer over the Gifts

Grant, Lord,
that as the self-offering of Christ, your Son,
has reconciled us to you,
so may the sacrifice of praise
keep us in joyful communion with you.
We ask this through Jesus Christ our Lord.

Eucharistic Preface

We lift up our hearts to you,
God of mercy and compassion;
to you we offer thanks and praise
through Jesus Christ your Son.

Though he was innocent,
he freely accepted suffering for the guilty
and he, the just one, bore an unjust sentence,
so that by his death we might be made righteous,
and through his resurrection,
we might be restored to peace with you.

And so, with angels and all saints
we glorify your holy name: Holy . . .

Prayer after Communion

Lord, let these holy gifts make us holy,
and prepare us to celebrate the Easter mystery.
We ask this through Christ our Lord.

PART TWO

PROPER TEXTS FOR THE WEEKDAYS OF LENT

These opening prayers, prayers over the gifts and prayers after Communion are translated and adapted from the Roman Missal to serve as appropriate prayers for a weekday Eucharist during Lent and Passiontide.

For the collects, a short conclusion is given. Longer conclusions may be used if desired.

A series of prefaces is also given, reflecting the themes of the Lenten season.

Thursday after Ash Wednesday

Opening prayer

Inspire our actions, Lord,
sustain them and grant them success;
so that in you may be found
the beginning and the end
of everything we undertake.
We ask this through Jesus Christ our Lord.

Prayer over the Gifts

Lord, as we prepare your table, we ask you
that the praise and fellowship offered here
may bring honour to your name
and reconciliation for your people.
Through Christ our Lord.

Prayer after Communion

You bless us, O God, with your heavenly gift,
and so with reverence we pray:
let this gift be for us
the source of your forgiveness and our salvation.
Through Christ our Lord.

Friday after Ash Wednesday

Opening prayer

God, our hope,
encourage us to persevere
in the works of penitence
which you have inspired in us,
so that with a pure heart we may accomplish
the Lenten observance we have begun.
We ask this through Jesus Christ our Lord.

Prayer over the Gifts

Lord, let a worthy observance of Lent
be the sacrifice of praise we offer,
and let the practice of self-denial
set us free to serve you.
We make this prayer through Christ our Lord.

Prayer after Communion

God, our saving help,
we pray that by this mystery
you will free us from sin
and make us responsive
to the healing power of your love.
Through Christ our Lord.

Saturday after Ash Wednesday

Opening prayer

Gracious God,
be pleased to look upon our weakness,
and so that we may not falter or fail,
let your right hand support and steady us.
We ask this through Jesus Christ our Lord.

Prayer over the Gifts

God of blessings,
give us words to utter
the sacrifice of praise
and hearts that live at peace with you.
We ask this through Christ our Lord.

Prayer after Communion

By heaven's own life you make us live
in the sharing of your sacrament, O God;
and so we ask that the living bread you give us
may make us ready to receive
the life of the age to come.
Through Christ our Lord.

First Monday

Opening prayer

God our Saviour,
turn us to yourself,
and instruct our minds in the lore of heaven,
so that through our keeping of Lent
we may learn to love you
and to love our neighbour for your sake.
We ask this through Jesus Christ our Lord.

Prayer over the Gifts

Father,
in the simplicity of Lent
we prepare your table.
Transform us into a people
whose life is your praise and glory.
We ask this through Christ our Lord.

Prayer after Communion

By receiving your sacrament, O God,
may we know you as the One who sets us free;
and in this freedom and healing from sin
let us rejoice both in body and spirit.
We ask this through Christ our Lord.

First Tuesday

Opening prayer

God of compassion,
look upon your family.
Set our heart firmly in your presence,
and while we endeavour to keep
to prayer, self-denial and works of love,
fill us with longing for your kingdom.
We make this prayer through Jesus Christ our Lord.

Prayer over the Gifts

God, creator of all things,
from the store of your great bounty
we set this table for your feast.
Let food that sustains us in this present time
be the spiritual food of eternal life.
We ask this through Christ our Lord.

Prayer after Communion

Through your sacrament, Lord God,
grant us this blessing:
that we may temper our desire for earthly goods
and learn to pursue the eternal good things
which you have prepared for those who are faithful.
We ask this through Christ our Lord.

First Wednesday

Opening prayer

God, source of every blessing,
stay close to us and keep us faithful to you,
and as we exercise moderation in our bodily needs,
refresh our hearts by the practice of good works.
We make this prayer through Jesus Christ our Lord.

Prayer over the Gifts

With your own gifts to us, O God,
we celebrate the fellowship of your table.
These gifts convey your grace in this present age;
we ask you to make them pledges of the age to come.
Through Christ our Lord.

Prayer after Communion

God, our provider,
you never cease to feed us by your sacraments.
Grant that the nourishment they impart to us
may bestow upon us eternal life.
This we ask through Christ our Lord.

First Thursday

Opening prayer

God, source of life,
we ask you to bestow on us
the spirit to think what is right
and promptly to perform it,
so that we, who without you can do nothing,
may be enabled to live according to your will.
Through Jesus Christ our Lord.

Prayer over the Gifts

Lord, in your compassion
hear the prayers of those who call upon you,
and, accepting us as we come to you,
turn our hearts completely to yourself.
We ask this through Christ our Lord.

Prayer after Communion

God, whose wisdom gives us the sacraments
to safeguard and strengthen the life of grace,
let this communion be a healing remedy for us
both now and in time to come.
We ask this through Christ our Lord.

First Friday

Opening prayer

God most holy,
make your people grow in readiness
to celebrate the coming feast of Easter,
so that the works of prayer, charity and self-denial
to which we have pledged ourselves

may bear fruit in both body and spirit.
We make this prayer through Jesus Christ our Lord.

Prayer over the Gifts

God of peace,
by the one sacrifice of Christ
you have reconciled us to yourself.
Accept us now as we celebrate that sacrifice
so that we may receive your gift of salvation.
We ask this through Christ our Lord.

Prayer after Communion

God, whose life springs ever new,
let this gift of your sacrament
free us from our old self,
that we may fully share in your salvation.
We ask this through Christ our Lord.

First Saturday

Opening prayer

Eternal God,
turn our hearts to you;
draw us to seek the one thing necessary
and arouse us to practise works of love,
so that we may be wholly dedicated
to your praise and glory.
We make this prayer through Jesus Christ our Lord.

Prayer over the Gifts

As we come to your table, Lord God,
teach us to bless your holy name
in everything we do and say.
This we ask through Christ our Lord.

Prayer after Communion

Tender God,
let your kindness
accompany those you nourish
by this holy sacrament,
and let your strength be the support of all
whom you have instructed in the ways of heaven.
We ask this through Christ our Lord.

Second Monday

Opening prayer

God, our wisdom,
you teach us to practise self-discipline,
for the renewal of body and spirit.
Bind us, we pray, by your word
and temper our hardness of heart,
that so bound, we may be truly free
and so tempered, we may practise
your commandment of selfless love.
We make this prayer through Jesus Christ our Lord.

Prayer over the Gifts

Gracious God, accept our prayers,
and free from earthly temptations
those you call into the communion
of your table on high.
We ask this through Christ our Lord.

Prayer after Communion

God our Father,
let this communion free us from sin
and make us partakers in your heavenly banquet.
We ask this through Christ our Lord.

Second Tuesday

Opening prayer

God, ever vigilant,
watch over your Church
with your perpetual steadfast love,
and since without you our human weakness falters,
support us, we beg you, free us from all harm,
and guide us to the things that will save us.
We make this prayer through Jesus Christ our Lord.

Prayer over the Gifts

In this sacrifice of praise, O God,
continue your holy work within us,
to purify us from earthly failings
and lead us to your heavenly gifts.
We ask this through Christ our Lord.

Prayer after Communion

God, our shepherd,
as we have eaten and drunk at your table,
nourish us in holiness
and bestow on us
the unfailing help of your mercy.
We ask this through Christ our Lord.

Second Wednesday

Opening prayer

Sustain your household, O God,
while you are training us
in your Lenten school of good works.
Be our support and comfort on earth,
and lead us in your mercy

to the blessings you promise us on high.
We make this prayer through Jesus Christ our Lord.

Prayer over the Gifts

Generous God,
amid the simplicity of Lent,
give us abundant blessings
through our communion at your table,
and make us abound
in the practice of good works.
We ask this through Christ our Lord.

Prayer after Communion

God, our provider,
you give us this sacrament
as a pledge of your eternal love.
Let it also strengthen us
to follow your law of love on earth.
This we ask through Christ our Lord.

Second Thursday

Opening prayer

O God, restorer and lover of innocence,
turn the hearts of your people to yourself.
Inspire us by your Spirit,
make us strong in faith
and effectual in good works.
We make this prayer through Jesus Christ our Lord.

Prayer over the Gifts

Lord, make our Lent holy
by this holy Eucharist,

and grant that the things
for which we offer thanks and praise
may work to good effect within us.
We ask this through Christ our Lord.

Prayer after Communion

All-powerful God,
let the Spirit of truth be strong among your people,
and as we share in the body and blood of Christ
fashion our lives in accordance with his gospel.
We ask this through Christ our Lord.

Second Friday

Opening prayer

God of all times and seasons,
through these holy forty days
create in us a clean heart,
a mind centred on truth
and a life lived in faithful love.
By these gifts prepare us
to celebrate your Easter feast
of new and risen life
in Christ our Lord,
who is alive, now and for ever.

Prayer over the Gifts

God of compassion, go before us always;
source of all goodness, make our lives good,
and, as you have called us to break bread with Christ,
keep us in the fellowship of those
who are dedicated to your will.
We ask this through Christ our Lord.

Prayer after Communion

Faithful God,
you give us the pledge of eternal salvation.
We pray you, guide our steps in your paths
and bring us at last to that promised goal.
We ask this through Christ our Lord.

Second Saturday

Opening prayer

God of glory,
you sustain us in this present age,
and make us partakers of the age to come.
Keep us faithful to you
in this life we now live,
so that we may be fit
to enter that eternal light
which is your dwelling place.
We make this prayer through Jesus Christ our Lord.

Prayer over the Gifts

Lord God,
we pray that as we offer the sacrifice of praise,
your grace may continue its work in us,
restraining our human intemperance
and leading us to salvation.
Through Christ our Lord.

Prayer after Communion

You know us, Lord, through and through.
Let the power of this sacrament
flood the inmost places of our heart
and make us able to receive

all that you want to give us.
This we ask through Christ our Lord.

Third Monday

Opening prayer

Gracious God,
let your boundless compassion
cleanse and sustain your Church,
and since without you it cannot stand,
support it and keep it faithful to your word.
We make this prayer through Jesus Christ our Lord.

Prayer over the Gifts

God, who call your unworthy servants
to be guests at your table,
let the bread of our service,
blessed and broken in Christ's hands,
be spiritual food to feed this world's hunger.
We ask this through Christ our Lord.

Prayer after Communion

Let our sharing in your sacrament, O God,
purify our hearts and gather us into unity.
We ask this through Christ our Lord.

Third Tuesday

Opening prayer

God, ever present,
do not allow your people
to be separated from you,

but bind us more closely to your service
and equip us always with your saving help.
We ask this through Jesus Christ our Lord.

Prayer over the Gifts

God of community,
you bid us eat and drink
according to the command of Christ.
Let this be the sacrifice
that binds us in obedience to him
and in fellowship with one another.
We ask this through Christ our Lord.

Prayer after Communion

God, our hope,
as we share in this holy mystery,
renew us in faith and service
and prompt us to express in the conduct of our lives
what here we celebrate in a sacred sign.
We ask this through Christ our Lord.

Third Wednesday

Opening prayer

God of all grace,
train us by Lenten observance
and nourish us by your word,
so that we may be bound to each other
in holy self-discipline
and united to you in steadfast prayer.
We ask this through Jesus Christ our Lord.

Prayer over the Gifts

Receive, O God, the prayers of your people
and the sacrifice of praise we are to offer.
Let this Eucharist be to us
healing, safety and the way to eternal life.
This we ask through Christ our Lord.

Prayer after Communion

God, at whose table we are fed,
let this feast make us holy,
free us from waywardness,
and render us worthy
of the eternal destiny you promise.
We ask this through Christ our Lord.

Third Thursday

Opening prayer

God of glory,
with reverence we ask you
that, as the day of our Saviour's resurrection approaches,
so we may prepare more eagerly
to celebrate his paschal mystery.
We make this prayer through Jesus Christ our Lord.

Prayer over the Gifts

God, source of all good,
keep far from your people
the infections of wickedness,
so that our sacrifice of praise may be acceptable to you.
We ask this through Christ our Lord.

Prayer after Communion

As you renew us by this sacrament, O God,
sustain us also by your kindly help,
so that we may lay hold of your saving work
both in these holy mysteries
and in the conduct of our life.
We ask this through Christ our Lord.

Third Friday

Opening prayer

Holy God,
strengthen your people in holiness.
Restrain us from intemperance
so that we may have the strength
to remain faithful to the law of heaven.
We make this prayer through Jesus Christ our Lord.

Prayer over the Gifts

Creator God,
look with favour
upon the fruits of human work
which we bring to prepare your table,
that they may be the food and drink of eternal life.
We ask this through Christ our Lord.

Prayer after Communion

All-powerful God,
let the working of your grace
fill our minds and bodies,
so that we may come to possess in fullest measure
the grace we now share in this holy sacrament.
We ask this through Christ our Lord.

Third Saturday

Opening prayer

God, in whom our joy is complete,
root us in the passion and resurrection of Christ,
so that we may know in its fullness
the happiness we now taste
through our observance of Lent.
We make this prayer through Jesus Christ our Lord.

Prayer over the Gifts

O God, whose gift it is
that we approach your mysteries
with our senses attuned to your presence,
grant, we pray,
that as we celebrate the Lord's Supper,
we may offer you the praise that is worthy of you.
Through Christ our Lord.

Prayer after Communion

God of abundance,
you nourish us plentifully with your holy gifts.
Open our hearts and minds
to what you have given us,
so that, having served you here,
we may live as bearers of your gospel.
This we ask through Christ our Lord.

Fourth Monday

Opening prayer

God of wonders,
in the great mystery of Easter

you promise the glory of all flesh.
Guide your Church in the ways
that you have set forth for our salvation,
so that as we journey towards your new age,
we may not lack your support
in this time of our pilgrimage.
We make this prayer through Jesus Christ our Lord.

Prayer over the Gifts

Lord God, we pray
that as we prepare your table
with praise and thanksgiving,
so you will prepare our hearts
to receive the joy of your kingdom.
We ask this through Christ our Lord.

Prayer after Communion

We pray you, O God,
that your holy gifts
may renew us in faith,
make us holy
and lead us to eternal life.
Through Christ our Lord.

Fourth Tuesday

Opening prayer

God of steadfast love,
keep us faithful
to the observance of Lent,
and so prepare us in heart and mind
to celebrate the Passover of Christ
in the joy of his rising from the dead.
We make this prayer through Jesus Christ our Lord.

Prayer over the Gifts

Creator God, we prepare your table
with the food you have given to support our earthly life.
Let it also be nourishment for life eternal.
This we ask through Christ our Lord.

Prayer after Communion

Lord, renew us in mind and heart
by this pledge of your heavenly banquet;
let us serve your peace and justice in this life,
so as to share the joy of the age to come.
We ask this through Christ our Lord.

Fourth Wednesday

Opening prayer

Righteous God,
you give a fitting recompense to the just
and pardon to sinners who repent.
Have mercy on us who cry out to you,
so that as we acknowledge our guilt,
we may be able to receive your forgiveness.
We make this prayer through Jesus Christ our Lord.

Prayer over the Gifts

God,
whose mercies are ever new,
transform our old self
in the sacrifice of praise,
and cause us to grow
in the new life which is your glory.
We ask this through Christ our Lord.

Prayer after Communion

God, physician of souls,
let those who receive your holy gifts
not be brought to judgement for sins,
but experience the grace of your sacrament
for peace, healing and new life.
This we ask through Christ our Lord.

Fourth Thursday

Opening prayer

Holy God,
you give the grace of repentance
to correct our sinful inclinations,
and you establish for us good works
to open our lives to the needy.
Make us persevere in your commandments
so that we may come without fault
to the celebration of our Passover in Christ,
who is alive, now and for ever.

Prayer over the Gifts

All-powerful God,
let the sacrifice of thanksgiving
bring your strength to our human weakness
and defend us from all that is evil.
We ask this through Christ our Lord.

Prayer after Communion

God, our help,
let the sacrament we have received
set us free from selfish inclinations
and break for us the shackles of guilt,

so that we may freely rejoice in your forgiveness.
We ask this through Christ our Lord.

Fourth Friday

Opening prayer

Generous God,
in prayer, self-denial and works of love
you provide the means to aid our human weakness;
make us pursue these things in simplicity and joy,
accepting them as your gracious gifts
and putting them into practice in the conduct of our lives.
We make this prayer through Jesus Christ our Lord.

Prayer over the Gifts

Almighty God,
let the table of Christ
nourish us in the life of the gospel,
so that with all our heart we may evermore abide in him.
We ask this through Christ our Lord.

Prayer after Communion

Grant, O God,
that this holy food and drink
may fortify us as we journey from old life to new,
so that we may lay aside our former ways
and be renewed in the Spirit of holiness.
We ask this through Christ our Lord.

Fourth Saturday

Opening prayer

God, the only source of life,
let the working of your mercy
direct the movement of our hearts,
since without your grace and guidance
we are unable to do what is just in your sight.
We make this prayer through Jesus Christ our Lord.

Prayer over the Gifts

Lord God,
open our lips in your praise,
and although our wilfulness rebels against you,
let the sacrifice of thanksgiving train us
to live a life that accords with your purpose.
This we ask through Christ our Lord.

Prayer after Communion

God, our provider,
let this holy food
change us, our hearts, minds and ways,
and make us worthy to be your children.
We ask this through Christ our Lord.

Fifth Monday

Opening prayer

God, by whose surpassing grace
we are made rich with all manner of blessings,
free us, we pray you, from our former ways
and lead us into newness of life,
that we may be prepared for the glory

of the heavenly kingdom.
Through Jesus Christ our Lord.

Prayer over the Gifts

All-holy God, we pray
that as we come to offer the sacrifice of thanksgiving
we may display the fruit of bodily penance
in joy and purity of mind and heart.
We ask this through Christ our Lord.

Prayer after Communion

Strengthened by the blessing of your sacraments
we pray you, O God,
that by these things
we may be turned away from sin
to follow the footsteps of Christ
and walk in the ways of your kingdom.
We ask this through Christ our Lord.

Fifth Tuesday

Opening prayer

God, whose desire it is
that all should come to know your truth,
keep your people faithful
in speaking your gospel of reconciliation,
so that many will be drawn to hear your word
and learn the ways of holiness and peace
in the communion of your Church.
We make this prayer through Jesus Christ our Lord.

Prayer over the Gifts

God, our peace,
we prepare your table
to share in the sacrifice of reconciliation.
Let your mercy turn us from our faults
and be the guide for our wavering hearts.
We ask this through Christ our Lord.

Prayer after Communion

God most high,
keep our hearts fixed
on your kingdom and your justice,
and by this holy sacrament
draw us ever nearer
to the blessings of heaven.
This we ask through Christ our Lord.

Fifth Wednesday

Opening prayer

God of mercy,
enlighten the hearts of your faithful people
whom you have consecrated
through the Lenten way of penance,
and as you have awakened in us
the desire to serve you in prayer,
receive our prayers with kindness
and answer them in love.
We make this prayer through Jesus Christ our Lord.

Prayer over the Gifts

God of abundance,
you prepare a table for us,

as a place where we may praise your name.
Let this feast be for your glory,
and a source of health and strength for your people.
We ask this through Christ our Lord.

Prayer after Communion

God, physician of souls,
let the gifts we have received
be for us a medicine from heaven,
to purge the evil in our hearts
and strengthen the good things
which you safeguard in us.
We ask this through Christ our Lord.

Fifth Thursday

Opening prayer

Be present, O God,
to those who call upon you,
and look with tender care
on those who place their hope in your mercy,
so that they may persevere without blame
in lives dedicated to holiness and justice,
and be made full heirs of your promise.
We make this prayer through Jesus Christ our Lord.

Prayer over the Gifts

God of community,
you invite us to share the table of Christ.
Shape our lives by his gospel,
as he breaks the bread of life
for the salvation of the whole world.
This we ask through Christ our Lord.

Prayer after Communion

Filled with your gift of salvation
we ask you, O God,
that as by a life-giving sacrament
you feed us in this present world,
so you will make us partakers
in the life that abides for ever.
Through Christ our Lord.

Fifth Friday

Opening prayer

God of patient love,
forgive the wrong that we have done,
so that by your goodness we may be released
from the sins that enslave us
and set free to serve you in peace.
We make this prayer through Jesus Christ our Lord.

Prayer over the Gifts

Gracious God,
let us offer a holy and worthy sacrifice of praise,
so that what we are to share
in the fellowship of your table
may be for our abiding salvation.
We ask this through Christ our Lord.

Prayer after Communion

God of justice,
let this holy feast
strengthen our resolve to reject the ways of sin
and embrace the new life of your gracious rule.
We ask this through Christ our Lord.

Fifth Saturday

Opening prayer

God of all times and seasons,
you are constantly at work
to bring about the salvation of humankind,
but in this time of Lent you offer your people
an even greater profusion of blessings.
Look kindly upon us,
strengthen those preparing for baptismal rebirth,
and grant new joy to those already reborn in baptism.
We ask this through Jesus Christ our Lord.

Prayer over the Gifts

God of new life,
in the sacrament of baptism
you make us one with the death of Christ
so that in his resurrection
we may live a new life.
Renew in us the joy of this faith,
inspire our thanksgiving
and fulfil our longing for your presence.
This we ask through Christ our Lord.

Prayer after Communion

With reverence we pray to you, O God,
that as you nourish us
with the communion of Christ's body and blood,
so you will make us partakers of the divine nature.
Through Christ our Lord.

Holy Week, Monday

Opening prayer

God, our hope,
look upon us in your compassion,
for we grow faint through human weakness.
Make us draw new breath
by the suffering and victory
of your Only-Begotten Son,
who is alive, now and for ever.

Prayer over the Gifts

Look graciously, O God,
upon these holy mysteries,
that as Christ by his passion
has cancelled the debt of our transgression,
so now as he breaks the bread for us
he may bring us to eternal life.
We ask this through Christ our Lord.

Prayer after Communion

God, ever present,
stand by your people
and with watchful kindness
keep us faithful to you,
that by your grace we may safeguard the gift
which your loving kindness has bestowed on us.
We ask this through Christ our Lord.

Holy Week, Tuesday

Opening prayer

All-powerful and eternal God,
grant us so to celebrate
the mystery of your Son's passion,
that we may experience your pardon and peace.
We make this prayer through Jesus Christ our Lord.

Prayer over the Gifts

Lord, look kindly on us
whom you gather at your table;
give us words to sing your praises
and let what you have begun in us
be nourished and brought to fulfilment.
We ask this through Christ our Lord.

Prayer after Communion

Filled with your saving gifts
we entreat your mercy, O God,
that through this sacrament
destined for our nourishment on earth,
you will make us partakers of eternal life.
We ask this through Christ our Lord.

Holy Week, Wednesday

Opening prayer

Gracious God,
who for our sake chose that your Son
should bear the yoke of the cross
to drive out the enemy's power from our midst;
grant that as we celebrate the suffering of Christ,

so we may participate in the grace of the resurrection.
We make this prayer in his name,
who is alive, now and for ever.

Prayer over the Gifts

As we come to your table, O God,
with reverence we ask you
to make effectual what we are to perform,
so that the passion of your Son
may consecrate us in holiness of mind, heart and body.
We ask this through Christ our Lord.

Prayer after Communion

Grant us, O God, to recognize
the wonder of this holy gift,
and as this communion bears witness
to the saving death of Christ your Son,
so it may fill us with the hope of eternal life
when he comes again in glory.
We ask this through Christ our Lord.

Eucharistic Prefaces for the Weekdays of Lent

Self-denial and charity

It is truly right and just for us
to glorify you, the all-powerful Father,
and offer you our song of thanksgiving and praise.

You desire us to express our thanksgiving
through works of self-denial,
to restrain our human pride
and by bringing relief to those in need
to imitate your generous compassion.

Therefore, with angels and saints,
we sing the unceasing hymn of your glory: Holy . . .

The return to Paradise

It is truly right and just, our duty and our salvation,
always and everywhere to give you thanks,
the all-holy God, our light and our redeemer.

Through Adam's greed in defying your command,
we had been justly cast out of Paradise;
now by the remedy of a fast
your grace has prevailed to call us back
to the blessedness of our ancient home,
and your love has taught us the commandments
by which we gain our freedom.

And so, with angels and saints
we glorify your holy name: Holy . . .

Lent, a gift from God

It is truly right and just, our duty and our salvation,
always and everywhere to give you thanks,
God, our light and our salvation.

You have given us this season of grace
to renew and purify our hearts and minds,
to set our hearts on the things that are eternal,
so as to live most fully for you in this present age.

Therefore, with angels and saints,
we exalt and glorify your holy name: Holy . . .

God, the merciful and compassionate One

We lift up our hearts to you,
the God of mercy and compassion,
as we offer you our song of thanks and praise.

In your kindness you absolve the repentant,
you restore to your friendship
the sinner who seeks your forgiveness,
and with great mercy you bestow the gift of eternal life
in Jesus, the Christ and Saviour.

And so, with every heavenly being
we glorify your holy name: Holy . . .

God who longs for his people to return

It is truly right and just for us to give you thanks,
to bless and praise you, here and everywhere,
God eternal, the Father of mercies.

You do not seek the death of sinners
but rather the passing of their sinfulness
and with great mercy and patience
you long for them to return to you.

And so, with angels and all saints
we glorify your holy name: Holy . . .

God restores us to innocence

It is truly right and just, our duty and our salvation,
always and everywhere to thank you,
the eternal and all-holy One.

You revive us in faith, build us up in hope
and join us in the bond of your love,
and when our conscience accuses us of guilt,
your freely given mercy restores us to innocence.

And so, with all the powers of creation,
we praise and adore you as we sing: Holy . . .

For Passiontide and Holy Week

It is truly right and just, our duty and our salvation,
to praise you, our God, and give you thanks
through Jesus Christ our Lord.

By the human nature he assumed,
he gathers us all into one body;
humbled, he raises us up,
handed over to die, he sets us free from death;
his suffering redeems us, his cross saves us,
his blood cleanses us, his flesh feeds us.

For this, we praise you, now and ever,
in the hymn of heaven as we sing: Holy . . .

PART THREE

PROPER TEXTS FOR THE THREE DAYS OF EASTER

Maundy Thursday evening till the evening of Easter Sunday

Easter, the Christian Passover, is a three-day festival comprising Good Friday, Holy Saturday and Easter Sunday of the Resurrection. Since Christians begin celebrating holy days at the previous evening's dusk, the 'Three Days of Easter' starts on Maundy Thursday evening with the Eucharist. The Three Days concludes with Evening Prayer of Easter Sunday.

The Easter Festival focuses on the 'Passover' of Jesus through death to the glory of the Father. Since the Middle Ages, both Catholics and Protestants have tended to see it as a series of separate 'historical' commemorations: the anniversary of Jesus' crucifixion followed by that of his resurrection two days later. A limited theology of atonement centred on the cross to the exclusion of the whole Passover event has contributed to this.

The older worship tradition familiar to the writers and preachers of the first Christian Millennium knows of no such limitations. All the services in the Three Holy Days are Easter services, because the 'Paschal Mystery' (the term rediscovered by the twentieth-century Liturgical Movement to describe the dying and rising of Christ) is one single saving event. Passion and Resurrection are inseparable. Nor is it merely historical. It is the Christian Passover, the Passover of Christ and the Passover of Christians 'in Christ' through faith and the sacraments to eternal life.

The evening Eucharist of Maundy Thursday, the Good Friday Liturgy of the Passion and the Vigil of Easter reflect the unity of the Paschal Mystery and should therefore be considered as one liturgical action spread over the three days. Together, this one act in three movements is the Christian Easter. Not until the end of the Easter Vigil Eucharist is the blessing given and the congregation dismissed.

In this section, texts are offered which are appropriate for use at the principal services of the three holy days. A second set of Good Friday solemn intercessions for the main service is given, together with an evening service for Good Friday and a Good Friday Procession, using the Passion according to Saint John. For the Easter Vigil, an alternative to the traditional Blessing of the Easter Candle is given and for Easter Sunday, in addition to the Eucharist (main service) provision, texts are suggested for an evening service in the form of a procession.

Maundy Thursday

The Evening Eucharist of the Lord's Supper

The Maundy Thursday Eucharist, while it commemorates the Institution of the Sacrament of the Lord's Supper and the washing of the disciples' feet by Jesus, should be seen as the first segment of the Three Day Easter sequence, rather than as a sort of independent eucharistic festival.

For this reason, the traditional chant to begin the Eucharist is taken from St Paul's letter to the Galatians, 6:14. A well-known English version of this is Isaac Watts' hymn (actually written for the Sacrament of the Lord's Supper) 'When I survey the wondrous cross', which might make a fitting beginning to the three holy days. Another version of the traditional chant is given below, to which the tune 'Rockingham' is also suitable. This verse should be used as a refrain between the verses of Psalm 67, sung to a suitable chant.

Proper texts

Introit (based on Galatians 6:14)

We glorify the cross of Christ,
We find our glory in his death,
In whom we die and rise to life,
Renewed and free, restored and whole.

Scripture-related opening prayers

Years ABC

By the blood of a lamb, O God,
you protected and saved your people;
and now, in the blood of your Son
you have reconciled the world to yourself.

Grant that, through our communion with Christ,
we may be faithful to his ministry of service,
so that at the last we may pass over joyfully
into the promised land of heaven.

We ask this through Jesus Christ,
who is one with you and the Holy Spirit,
for ever and ever.

or:

God, our wisdom,
in the cross of Christ you unmask our violence
and execute judgement on the idols we serve.

As we break the bread in thanksgiving
and share the cup of blessing together,
make known among us your will for peace,
for reconciliation and mutual service,
that your rule may be welcomed
and our joy be complete.

We ask this through Jesus Christ,
who is one with you and the Holy Spirit,
now and for ever.

Opening prayer

God of mercy,
bestow on all your faithful people
new life through the passion of your Son.
Let the Eucharist which he gave us
teach us to love one another
and to serve our neighbour
in the charity of Christ.
We ask this in his name,
our Saviour, now and for ever.

Acclamation
Philippians 2:6–11

V/: Christ was humbler yet
even to accepting death,
death on a cross.
But God raised him high
and gave him the name
that is above all other names.

Intercession

God, our Father,
listen to the prayer of your Son,
that your people may be consecrated in the truth
even as he consecrated himself
for the life of the world.
For he is alive, now and for ever.

Prayer over the Gifts

Gracious God,
make us worthy to celebrate
the Supper of the Lord,
for as often as we do this
to celebrate his sacrifice,

the work of our redemption is made present.
We make this prayer through Christ, our Lord.

Eucharistic Preface

It is truly right and just, our duty and our salvation,
always and everywhere to give you thanks,
Lord, holy Father, almighty and eternal God,
through Jesus Christ our Lord.

Christ is the true and eternal priest
who established for us
the form and pattern of the eternal sacrifice.
For he gave himself, his body and blood,
and in the Eucharist, taught us to enter
into the movement of his self-offering.
And so, when we eat the bread and drink the cup
we celebrate his saving Passover
until he returns in glory.

Therefore, with all the powers of heaven
we glorify your holy name: Holy . . .

Prayer after Communion

Sustain us, O God, here on earth
by the Supper of the Lord
and through this food make us hungry
for the feast you have prepared
in your kingdom.
We ask this through Christ our Lord.

Reserving the consecrated gifts

If some of the consecrated bread (and wine) is to be reserved for
the service of Good Friday, it may be taken in procession to its
place of reservation, which should be prepared so as to allow

people to remain there in prayer and vigil. Hymns recalling the Last Supper are suitable for the procession.

Maundy Thursday: The Washing of Feet

This rite seems to have originated in monastic communities, though Saint Ambrose records that he was accustomed to wash the feet of those baptized at Easter. The rite may be done during the Maundy Thursday Eucharist, after the sermon and before the Intercession, or as a separate act of worship.

Some churches understand the rite as a sort of play of Jesus washing the disciples' feet. However, it is more consistent with the origins of the ceremony to regard it as a symbolic act of service, by which the Church renews its commitment to serve the world in the charity of Christ, its members having first enacted service of one another.

As such, there is no limit to the number of those whose feet might be washed. Small congregations might wash each other's feet throughout the church. However it is done, the rite should be visible to everyone in the church.

If the Washing of Feet is done at the Eucharist, the president should end the homily with words introducing this rite. Then the president takes off the outer vestments and wraps a towel round the waist. Assistants follow with bowl, warm water and towels.

Suitable anthems, psalms and hymns are sung. The rite may end with this prayer:

Prayer

Christ, our brother,
bless this act of humble service;
and as you were pleased to wash your disciples' feet,
so let what we have done together here
teach us the ministry of serving others
even as you have come among us,
not to be served, but to serve.

For you are our teacher and example
now and for ever.

Maundy Thursday: *The Stripping of the Altar*

After the Eucharist, the ministers may return to the altar and, perhaps also with the help of the congregation, remove the cloths and hangings from the altar and its surroundings. Psalm 22 might be recited or sung during this ceremony. For Good Friday the altar should be completely bare.

Maundy Thursday: *The watch at the place of reservation*

A silent watch may be kept. If the time is prolonged, then at intervals, some readings may be required. Passages of the Gospel of John are appropriate, such as selections from John 14—17 (The Last Discourse) and John 17 (Jesus' high priestly prayer), or selections from the Passion narratives of the Synoptic Gospels.

Suitable songs may be sung. Taizé chants are very suitable. Some of those suggested for the reading of the Passion on Palm Sunday may be used here.

Some prayers that may be used:

Father,
you have entrusted everything
into your Son's hands,
and he gives himself up
that we may be consecrated in the truth.
As we accompany him in vigil,
keep us awake,
save us from the time of trial,
and deliver us out of darkness
into the light of his resurrection,
for you have loved us for ever and ever.

Father,
you heard the prayer of Christ,
offered in conflict and agony
as he accepted the fullness of his mission.
Now, risen from death, he intercedes for us.
Let his prayer keep your people watchful,
his tears enlarge our hearts
and his obedience renew our strength
as we attempt to walk the way of the cross
in the light of his risen life.
We ask this in his name,
our Saviour, now and for ever.

Holy God,
Even in this hour of darkness,
in the grief and anguish of your Son,
you display your fathomless love.
For you did not abandon your beloved,
and the evil one did not prevail over him.
Give us the strength to watch and pray with Christ,
that we may not enter into temptation.
Lead us to the dawn of that day
when the work of your glory will be accomplished,
for ever and ever.

Merciful God,
we keep vigil, in awe and trembling,
before you this night.
For in the hours of this world's darkness
the fearsome conflict is begun
between Life itself and the powers of death.
Do not let us lose heart
as we contemplate the evils of our age,
but open our eyes to the resurrection of Christ,
in which already we may perceive the dawning
of that great and final day
when you are all in all,
for ever and ever.

Here, O God,
we watch and pray with Christ,
as he, in his agony, sets himself to do your will.
Death will consume him,
yet death itself will be consumed
as he rises in triumph from the grave.
Through these dark hours,
keep the light of faith burning in our hearts
so that we may venerate his cross as the tree of life.
Grant, that even as we grieve for his dying,
we may rejoice that he has accomplished all things
and comes to greet us with his risen peace,
who is alive, now and for ever.

The Vigil might end with Compline, which should be recited as usual, although if a proper final collect is required, this may be used:

Collect

Send us in peace, Lord,
to rest in safety and confidence
beneath the arms of the cross,
by which you have reconciled
the world to yourself
We ask this through Christ our Lord.

Good Friday

The Liturgy of the Passion

The Liturgy of Good Friday traditionally has four elements: first, the Ministry of the Word, secondly, the Solemn Intercession for the Church and for the world, thirdly, the Veneration of the Cross, and fourthly, Holy Communion ministered from the consecrated bread and wine reserved after the Eucharist of Maundy Thursday.

However, different views are held as to the appropriateness of all these elements and of their order. Some churches keep the Solemn Intercession until the end of the service, some do not administer Communion, others adopt various procedures for the Veneration, or 'Proclamation', of the Cross.

To allow for these differing approaches, the texts offered here follow the traditional Latin pattern: Word, Intercession, Veneration of the Cross, Holy Communion. However, the juxtaposition of one or other element, or the omission of others, may be done without significantly departing from the integrity of the service, provided that the Ministry of the Word comes first.

It might be useful to remember some points that are often raised concerning the Liturgy for Good Friday.

As the second segment of the Easter Festival, the Good Friday Liturgy is a celebration of the Cross as the Tree of Life. The Passion Narrative of the Fourth Gospel is proclaimed. This emphasizes the triumphant exaltation of the Son of Man, who at the culmination of the days of his flesh fulfils in his own body the Passover event, announces the accomplishment of God's work and breathes forth the Spirit.

However, it is also situated in the middle of what was once kept as a period of fasting, lasting from Maundy Thursday evening until the end of the Easter Vigil. In this period, there was no Eucharist, since its celebration would have broken the fast. That is why it is traditional not to celebrate the Eucharist between the Mass of the Last Supper and the Easter Vigil.

These two facts suggest that thought needs to be given, first, to how the 'Proclamation of the Cross' is handled, and second, to whether Communion on this day is appropriate.

As to the form of the cross, it is clear from the origins and ancient texts of the Rite that this cross will have no figure of the crucified Christ upon it. Effectively, the Good Friday Cross speaks of the resurrection. It should therefore be empty.

However, empty should not mean bare. The Cross is celebrated not as a gallows but as the tree of life, set in the midst of the new Paradise, whose branches bear a healing fruit. The design of the Good Friday Cross should reflect this. Preparing the cross is a moment for the creative imagination, a time to take lessons from the many portrayals of the Cross in early Christian art, where it becomes a form of beauty and glory, the sign of the One who is victorious.

The service begins in silence with the entry of the ministers. It is traditional for the president and ministers to prostrate themselves before the altar and keep silence for a few moments. All then stand. The Opening Prayer or Collect is then said without any introduction.

Scripture-related opening prayer

Accomplished, O God,
is the work of our redemption:
for the Lamb is slain,
and the Passover prepared anew;
the blood and water have flowed
to sanctify a people consecrated to your name.

Grant that we, who celebrate
the One who was lifted up,
may find in him true wisdom,
healing for our wounds
and help in time of need.

We ask this through Jesus Christ,
who is one with you and the Holy Spirit,
for ever and ever.

Opening prayer

God, our glory,
by the passion of Christ your Son
you have abolished the death
which was our ancient inheritance.
Form us afresh in your image,

so that we who by nature
are formed to bear the likeness of earth,
may be transformed by grace
to bear the likeness of heaven, in Jesus Christ,
who is one with you and the Holy Spirit,
now and for ever.

Acclamation
Philippians 2:6–11

V/: Christ was humbler yet
even to accepting death,
death on a cross.
But God raised him high
and gave him the name
that is above all other names.

The sermon will follow the proclamation of the Passion.

The Solemn Intercession

The Intercession consists of biddings, periods of silent prayer and
collects. The biddings are spoken by the president or deacon
or other minister; the whole congregation keeps silence. The
president speaks the collect.

It is proper for the congregation to stand. After the Bidding,
however, the congregation may be invited to kneel for a brief
silence before standing again for the collect. The deacon or
another minister may say *Let us kneel*. After a short pause, the
minister may say *Let us rise*.

Other ways of marking the prayer of the people after the
Bidding might be devised. For example, the Taizé response 'O
Lord, hear my prayer' might be sung while the people are kneel-
ing. Or during each silent pause (or during the singing), a member of the congregation or server may place a lighted candle on a
stand in the midst of the congregation.

Proper texts

The president begins the Intercession:

My dear friends in Christ,
let us offer our solemn prayer.

A deacon or other minister may continue:

First of all, let us pray for the Church:
may God give it peace and unity throughout the world,
so that we may live in tranquillity and give glory to God.

Collect

Almighty and eternal God,
in Christ you have revealed your glory
to the whole world.
Continue, we pray you, this work of your mercy
and keep your Church faithful
in its confession of your name.
Through Christ our Lord.

Let us pray for N. our Bishop,
that God who set him apart
as Shepherd of this Church
may keep him safe and sound.

Collect

Almighty and eternal God,
whose law is the foundation of all things,
we pray you, in your mercy safeguard N. our Bishop,
so that under your constant care
your flock may grow and mature in faith.
Through Christ our Lord.

Let us pray for all who serve
as bishops, priests, and deacons;

for all ministers in the Church,
and all the holy people of God.

Collect

Almighty and eternal God,
by whose Spirit the body of your Church
is guided, governed and made holy;
hear our prayer for all orders of ministry
and bestow your gifts upon all your people,
that we may bear the fruit of faithful service.
Through Christ our Lord.

*If the prayer for governments, below, p. 84, is used, this bidding
and collect should be omitted.*

Let us pray for Elizabeth our Queen,
for those who serve our nation in government,
for all who make and uphold our laws
and all who serve the needs of our communities.

Collect

Almighty and eternal God,
whose rule is justice, love and peace;
remember, we pray you, Elizabeth our Queen,
those in public office
and all who support our national life,
that good government and irreproachable service
may draw us to live in harmony with one another.
Through Christ our Lord.

Let us pray for those
who are preparing for Baptism,
and all who are learning to be Christians.
May God open their ears to the Word,
give them new life in the waters of rebirth

and number them with believers
in Christ Jesus the Lord.

Collect

Almighty and eternal God,
by whose gift the Church is made fruitful
with new offspring,
grant to all who are preparing for baptism
a deeper faith and understanding,
so that born again in the saving waters,
they may be counted among your adopted children.
Through Christ our Lord.

Let us pray for Christian unity;
for all our brothers and sisters who believe in Christ,
that God may make all of us one,
and keep us together in one holy Church.

Collect

Almighty and eternal God,
whose will it is that all believers
be gathered and united in Christ,
we beg you to look upon the flock
your Son has redeemed,
and as we share one baptism,
draw us together in the service
of one Christian faith.
Through Christ our Lord.

Let us pray for the Jewish people,
the first to hear the word of God;
that God may safeguard them in reverence
for the holy Name revealed to them,
and keep them faithful to the Covenant.

The Three Days of Easter

Collect

Almighty and eternal God,
whose promise was made to Abraham and Sarah
and to their descendants for ever;
we pray you in your mercy
to heed the prayer of your Church,
that as you chose them as your holy people,
so you will lead them to the fullness of redemption.
Through Christ our Lord.

Let us pray for those who do not believe in Christ,
that the light of the Holy Spirit
may guide them into the way of salvation.

Collect

Almighty and eternal God,
grant, we pray,
that those who do not believe in Christ
may find the truth by walking before you
in sincerity of heart.
Make your people grow in love,
eager to receive more fully
the mystery of your life
and be more effective witnesses to you.
Through Christ our Lord.

Let us pray also for those who do not believe in God,
that they may wholeheartedly seek truth and right,
and so be led to God.

Opening prayer

Almighty and eternal God,
who created all men and women
to desire you, and so to find you;

to find you, and so to be at peace in you;
grant, we pray, that your love and care
may reach those who do not acknowledge you,
and let the witness of believers
remove all obstacles to belief,
so that all may rejoice in you,
the one true God, our Creator.
Through Christ our Lord.

The following should be omitted if the prayer for the Queen is used.

Let us pray for all who govern the nations,
that God may guide their hearts and minds
to follow his purposes for peace and justice
and the freedom of all humanity.

Collect

Almighty and eternal God,
whose hand protects all men and women
and safeguards the rights of all;
look kindly on those
who bear the burden of government,
and grant by your gracious gift,
that peoples everywhere may prosper
and live in freedom to worship you.
Through Christ our Lord.

Finally, dear friends in Christ,
let us pray God the all-powerful Father,
to drive out falsehood from the world,
to remove the scourge of sickness and hunger,
bring freedom to the oppressed,
safe passage and happy homecoming to the traveller,
health to the sick and salvation to the dying.

Collect

Almighty and eternal God,
our comfort in grief, our strength in affliction;
let the cries of those who suffer
ring loud in the ears of your compassion,
that all may rejoice in your saving help,
and experience your constant love.
We make this prayer
through Jesus Christ our Lord.

An alternative set of prayers for the Intercession may be found on p. 101.

The Service of the Cross

This part of the Liturgy consists of the displaying of the cross and the response of the congregation. Two forms are possible for displaying the cross.

First Form: a Procession

The cross to be used is prepared at the back of the church. The president (or the deacon), accompanied by servers or members of the congregation carrying (incense and) lighted candles, takes up the cross and proceeds a little way up the middle of the main aisle, where the first halt is to be made. A cantor sings:

V/. This is the wood of the Cross,
 where hung the Saviour of the world:
R/. O come, and let us worship.
All may kneel in silence for a few moments.

The procession makes a second halt in the middle of the church, when the proclamation is made a second time. Again all may kneel.

A third and final halt is made at the chancel step, where the call and response is made one more time. The cross is placed in a location where it may be clearly seen and where, if appropriate, the congregation may come to venerate it.

Second Form: Unveiling

Before the Liturgy begins, the cross should be standing in the middle of the church, if this can be done without impeding the movement of the people. Any prominent and accessible location will be suitable. The cross should be completely shrouded in red cloth.

The president (or the deacon) goes in procession to the cross and partially removes the cloth. The cantor sings the verse, to which the people reply. All kneel for a short time.

The cloth is further drawn back, with call and response as before, and the people may kneel again.

A third and final time, the cloth is allowed to fall away, the response is made and the people kneel.

The People's Response

In some congregations, people may wish to come forward to venerate the cross. For this purpose, it should either be laid flat on the floor, or on a low platform or ramp. During the veneration, suitable anthems, psalms or hymns should be sung.

An anthem to be sung between verses of Psalm 67 ('Rockingham' is a suitable melody)

We glorify your Cross, O Lord,
Your resurrection we proclaim;
For by this holy, blessed wood,
Your joy has come to all the world.

The Reproaches

The 'Reproaches' are a cry modelled on that of the Prophets, particularly Micah and Hosea, against an unfaithful people. The version given below is for two voices and chorus. It should be sung, and is best chanted to a simple psalm chant.

Chant for the first four lines:

V/. O my people! What have I done to you?
How have I displeased you? Answer me!
I led you out of Egypt,
from slavery to freedom:

Chant for the second four lines:

V/. Christ is led to the Cross,
led like a lamb to the slaughter,
mute and wordless before his enemies,
never opening his mouth.

Refrain:

V/. O my people! What have I done to you?
How have I displeased you? Answer me!
I led you through the desert forty years
and fed you with manna from heaven:

V/. Christ is led to the Cross,
despised and rejected by all,
oppressed, abused and afflicted,
struck with a reed and crowned with thorns.

R/. God most holy,
God most mighty,
God immortal, have mercy on us.

V/. What more could I have done for you?
As my beautiful vine I planted you,
hoping that you would yield abundant vintage,
but sour grapes were all your harvest.

V/. Christ is led to the Cross,
poison is his food to eat,
and in his parching thirst
vinegar is all he has to drink.

R/. God most holy,
God most mighty,
God immortal, have mercy on us.

V/. O my people! What have I done to you?
How have I displeased you? Answer me!
I sent plagues to scourge your captors,
my angel to destroy their firstborn.

V/. Christ is led to the Cross,
wounded for our transgressions,
the firstborn of creation,
cut off from the land of the living.

R/. God most holy,
God most mighty,
God immortal, have mercy on us.

V/. I led you from slavery to freedom;
Your oppressors I put to confusion;
I opened wide the sea before you,
to make a road for you to pass.

V/. Christ hangs on the wood of the Cross,
the One in whom is the fullness of God
is emptied of power, dying like a slave;
and his side is opened with a spear.

R/. God most holy,
God most mighty,
God immortal, have mercy on us.

V/. O my people, remember now:
the tree whose fruit you ate and tasted death;
the blood that saved you from the deadly plague;
my steadfast love which never fails.

V/. Christ has borne our sins in his body on the Tree,
that we might die to sin and live to righteousness;
by his wounds we have been healed,
by his blood, we are reconciled to God.

R/. God most holy,
God most mighty,
God immortal, have mercy on us.

The cross is left in front of the altar or in another place where it may be clearly visible. Lighted candles are placed either side of the cross.

The Service of Communion

The bread and wine required are brought from the place of reservation and placed on the altar. This should be done in silence and without ceremony.

The Lord's Prayer is said and the people invited to Communion in the usual way.

After Communion, these two prayers are used to end the service. There is no blessing or dismissal. If there is no distribution of Communion, the first prayer is not used.

Prayer after Communion

All-powerful God,
you have restored us to life
by the triumphant death and rising of Christ.
Let your gracious work
be continued and grow in us,
that we who share in these holy things
may never cease to give you praise.
We ask this through Jesus Christ our Lord.

Final prayer

Let your abundant blessing, O God,
be poured upon your people
who have celebrated the death of your Son
in the hope of the resurrection.
Come to us with your forgiveness,
uplift us with your consolation,
deepen your faith in our hearts
and bring us to eternal redemption.
We ask this through Christ our Lord.

Good Friday: An Evening Service around the Cross

The Taizé community introduced this form of prayer and it has become popular in many churches. For this service, the large cross that was used at the Liturgy of the Passion should be used. It should lie on the church floor, supported a few inches off the floor or on a shallow ramp. People should sit around the cross.

Candles and other lights should be lit around the cross. Other lighting should be minimal.

Incense might be used during the Preparation or Intercession parts of the service. For this, a large bowl should be filled with dry sand and a small metal dish placed in the middle for the charcoal. The bowl should stand by the cross, on the floor or a low stand. The congregation might be invited to place grains of incense on the burning charcoal.

For the Preparation, Taizé chants may be used. Plenty of time should be given for this. The source references here are to *Taizé 2002–2003*. Particularly suitable are:

20 Adoramus te Christe
26 La tenebre (Our darkness is never darkness in your sight)
30 In manus tuas
32 Mon âme se repose (In God alone my soul can find rest and peace)
37 Jesus remember me
47 Per crucem
48 Crucem tuam
60 O Christe Domine Jesu

The last part of the Passion Story is read: John 19:41–42. This might be chanted using the traditional tone:

John 19:41– 42

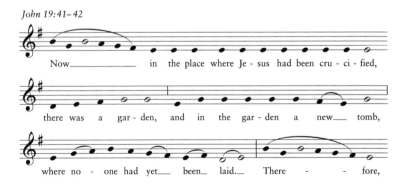

Now _____ in the place where Je - sus had been cru - ci - fied, there was a gar - den, and in the gar - den a new__ tomb, where no - one had yet__ been__ laid.__ There - - fore,

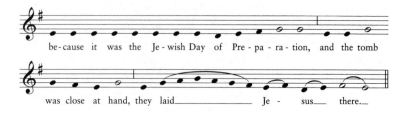

be-cause it was the Je-wish Day of Pre - pa - ra - tion, and the tomb
was close at hand, they laid_____ Je - sus_ there._

Psalm 143 may be sung, using this refrain:

In the dark-ness you have laid_ me, like the dead of long a - go.

Tone for the psalm:

A period of silent prayer may now be kept.

Then people might be invited to come to the cross and touch it, or place a lighted candle by its side. If they have special requests for prayer, people to be remembered, etc., these may be spoken out loud. Plenty of time should be allowed for this.

Music could be played or sung during this time of intercession.

When everyone is settled again, the service concludes with the Lord's Prayer and this Collect may be used:

Faithful God,
look upon your people,
for whose sake our Saviour Jesus Christ
accepted betrayal, rejection
and death upon the Cross;
who now in glory pleads for us,
for ever and ever.

A Procession of the Passion for Good Friday

The Passion Narrative according to John moves from the garden across the Kidron Valley, via the High Priest's House to the Roman Government Headquarters, to Golgotha and to another garden, where Jesus' body is laid.

In this service, the Passion is proclaimed in procession. It is divided into seven sections, each one representing a halt on the processional path. The order given below is an outline. At each halt there may be mime or dramatization, and/or intercessions may be made.

The whole space of the church building should be used for this service. Seven stands will be needed where the procession is to halt, with enough room for everyone to gather round. Each stand should be decorated appropriately.

Alternatively, this service might be celebrated outside the church, as a street procession or act of witness.

Banners should be made to lead the procession. They might appropriately have representations of the Instruments of the Passion (the nails, spear, cross, crown of thorns, etc.), and crowns, since the note of the Passion is one of triumph. The readers carry the books from which the Passion is to be read; they should be accompanied by lighted candles and incense if appropriate.

In the procession a large decorated cross, without the figure of the crucified Christ, should be carried.

The people gather.

During the gathering, suitable songs or Taizé chants may be sung to allow people to orient themselves for prayer.

The president and ministers enter informally during the gathering and take their seats, so that they may share in the gathering prayer.

When the time comes to begin the service, the ministers rise. The president may say some words of introduction to the service. a silence is kept, after which the president recites the opening prayer.

Opening prayer

God, our glory,
by the passion of Christ your Son
you have abolished the death
which was our ancient inheritance.
Form us afresh in your image,
so that we who by nature
are formed to bear the likeness of earth,
may be transformed by grace
to bear the likeness of heaven, in Jesus Christ,
who is one with you and the Holy Spirit,
now and for ever.

Those who are to read the Passion go to the president and ask for a blessing. The president says:

May the word of God
be on your lips
and the Spirit of the Holy One
be in your hearts.

The president turns to the congregation and says:

May God bless us who listen,
and raise our heart to be with Christ
who has accomplished all this for our salvation.

R/. Amen.

The Procession begins with the hymn 'The royal banners forward go' (New English Hymnal 79) or another suitable processional song, during which it goes to the first halt.

The Three Days of Easter

The first reader announces the Passion:

Reader: The Passion of the Lord Jesus Christ according to John.

John 18:1–11 is read.

A short silence may be kept. Then this canticle, based on Isaiah 52–53, is sung:

Refrain:

Lamb of God, you take a - way the sins of the world; have mer - cy on us.

Tone for the verses:

Verses:
Who has believed what we have heard?
To whom has the Lord revealed his power?
For like a young plant he grew up before him,
like a root out of dried-up earth.

He was not handsome, that we should look at him,
nor beautiful, that we should desire him;
he was despised and rejected,
filled with sorrow, a friend of grief.

Yet it was our sorrow he was bearing,
our griefs he carried;
and we, we saw him as stricken,
smitten by God and afflicted.

But he was wounded for our transgressions,
bruised for our iniquities;
his was the punishment that made us whole,
and by his wounds we have been healed.

Suitable alternatives are 'The Servant' (in Enemy of Apathy, Iona Community *1988), Brian Foley's hymn 'See, Christ was wounded for our sake' or Timothy Dudley-Smith's 'No weight of gold or silver' (*Hymns for Today's Church *137 and 138).*

A time of silent prayer may be kept.

This Collect may be used:
In a garden, O God,
we took our own way
and lost your friendship;
now in this garden,
one who is our flesh and blood
has pledged himself
to take your way, even unto death.
Teach us how to be faithful
as Christ your Son was faithful,
that we may truly be your children.
We ask this through Jesus Christ:
R/. Amen.

The Procession moves to the second halt, at the House of Annas.

John 18:12–27 is read.

*A short silence may be kept. The hymn 'Ah, holy Jesu' (*New English Hymnal *62) may be sung, or Christopher Idle's 'He stood before the court' (*Hymns for Today's Church *129).*

This Collect may be used:
God, whose Son,
though innocent, was tried as guilty,
and found to deserve death;
let all who are unjustly accused
be given the words to answer injustice
with the power of love,
as followers of Christ.
We ask this in his name:
R/. Amen.

The procession moves to the third halt, the Headquarters of Pilate.

John 18:28–40 is read.

*A short silence may be kept. The hymn 'My song is love unknown' (*New English Hymnal *86) or the Lent Prose (*New English Hymnal *507) may be sung.*

This Collect may be used:
God, you so loved the world
that you gave your only Son:
the innocent in exchange for the guilty,
the blameless One in the place of the sinner.
As Christ has taken his stand with us in being human,
so fashion us after the likeness of your humanity.
We ask this in his name.
R/. Amen.

The procession moves to the fourth halt, the Soldiers' Hall.

John 19:1–16 is read.

A short silence may be kept. The Song 'O Lord my God' (in Enemy of Apathy*) may be sung, or the hymn 'A purple robe, a crown of thorns' (*Hymns for Today's Church *122).*

This Collect may be used:
God of glory,
you did not hide your Christ
from beatings and ridicule;
steady your people,
and give them patience
when they are called
to suffer injustice
because they are Christ's disciples.
We ask this in his name.
R/. Amen.

Proper texts

The procession goes to the fifth halt, the Way of the Cross.

John 19:16b–25 is read.

A short silence may be kept. The canticle from Philippians 2:5–11 may be sung:

Je - sus Christ— is Lord, to the glo - ry of God the Fa - ther.

Tone for the verses:

Though he was in the form of God,
Jesus did not regard equality with God as something to be exploited;
but emptied himself, taking the form of a slave
being born in human likeness.

And being found in human form he humbled himself
and became obedient to the point of death, even death on a cross.
Therefore God also highly exalted him
and gave him the name that is above every name,

So that at the name of Jesus every knee should bend,
in heaven and on earth and under the earth,
and every tongue should confess that Jesus Christ is Lord
to the glory of God the Father.

Alternatives are the song 'He is Lord' (Hymns for Today's Church S.7), or 'Empty he came' (Hymns for Today's Church 127)

This Collect may be used:
God, whose purpose it was
that your Christ should carry the cross

to expel from our midst
the power of our ancient enemy;
let the enemy be killed in us
by the power of that same cross,
that we may live
in the light of Christ's resurrection.
We ask this in his name.
R/. Amen.

The procession moves to the sixth halt, the Cross.

John 19: 25b–37 is read.

*The hymn 'O come and stand beneath the cross' (*New English Hymnal 98*) may be sung. Alternatively, the song 'Lord Jesus Christ, shall I stand still' (in* Enemy of Apathy*) may be used.*

This Collect may be used:
God, who in the crucifixion of your Christ
reached out your hands
to embrace all men and women;
let us not refuse
the love which created and sustains us,
but make us practise it
in care for our neighbour's need,
according to Christ's command.
We ask this in his name.
R/. Amen.

or this:

God, the origin and end of all,
you delivered everything
into the hands of your Christ
in whose death your purpose is accomplished.
Grant that through the Passover of Christ
all humanity may pass
from darkness into light

and from this world to you.
We ask this in his name,
who is alive, now and for ever.
R/. Amen.

The procession moves to the seventh halt, Joseph of Arimathaea's Tomb.

John 19:38–42 is read.

*The song 'Were you there when they crucified my Lord?' (*New English Hymnal 93*), or alternatively, 'With Christ we share a mystic grave' (*New English Hymnal 317*) or the Taizé response 'Mon âme se repose – In God alone my soul can find rest and peace' may be used.*

This Collect may be used:
God, our life,
from whose love
neither death nor the grave
will separate us;
give us the patience to wait
and the courage to encounter darkness,
knowing that in the resurrection of Jesus
there is the dawn of a new and unending day.
We ask this in his name,
who is alive, now and for ever.

*The procession returns to the sanctuary, while the hymn 'Praise to the Holiest' (*New English Hymnal 439*) is sung.*

The service ends with the Collect:

Accomplished, O God,
is the work of our redemption:
for the Lamb is slain,
and the Passover prepared anew;

the blood and water have flowed
to sanctify a people consecrated to your name.
Grant that we, who celebrate
the One who was lifted up,
may find in him true wisdom,
healing for our wounds,
and help in time of need.
We ask this through Jesus Christ,
who is one with you and the Holy Spirit,
for ever and ever.

The congregation departs in silence.

Good Friday

An alternative for the Solemn Intercession in the Liturgy of Good Friday

Some or all of these biddings and prayers may be used instead of those given above, p. 85.

For the whole Church:

Let us pray for the Church, God's people,
called into fellowship with Christ as his members
and animated by the Holy Spirit.

Collect

God of the Covenant,
you gather a people to yourself
from all the nations,
and you make that people one by your Holy Spirit.
Keep your Church faithful to its mission,
that it may truly be a life-giving leaven
for the whole human family
to serve and renew it in Christ.

We ask this in his name,
our Saviour, now and for ever.

For the spread of the gospel:

Let us pray that the Good News of Christ
may be heard and received throughout the world,
so that God's name may be praised by all nations.

Collect

God, whose will it is
that all should be saved
and come to the knowledge of your truth;
send your disciples as workers in your harvest
to preach the gospel to every nation,
so that from the rising of the sun to its setting
a pure offering may be made to your name.
We ask this in the name of Christ,
our Saviour, now and for ever.

For the unity of Christians:

Let us pray for Christian unity,
for an end to our divisions,
for truth, tolerance and faith in the one God.

Collect

God, in whose threefold life
all Christians are called to share;
make and keep us one,
that, as there is one Christ and one baptism,
so we may show to the world
that unity in truth and action
which is your desire for us.
We ask this in the name of Christ,
our Saviour, now and for ever.

For our nation:

Let us pray for our nation,
for civil peace and harmony,
for good and honest public servants
and goodwill between communities.

Collect

God of wisdom,
whose rule sets all things in order;
guide our nation in the ways of justice and peace;
let our rulers be wise and our citizens just,
let the frail be supported
and the powerful encouraged to do right;
let there be respect between communities
and tolerance among us all.
We ask this in the name of Christ,
our Saviour, now and for ever.

For the poor and oppressed:

Let us pray for those in poverty,
and those who live under oppression,
that their rights may be upheld
and their needs addressed.

Collect

God, lover of the poor,
you hear the cries of the oppressed
and set the downtrodden free.
Grant to those with abundant means
the grace to minister to the needy,
and confront the arrogance of the oppressor
with the gentle power of the gospel.
We ask this through Jesus Christ,
our Saviour, now and for ever.

For peace and justice:

Let us pray for peace and justice,
for those who work for peace,
that humankind, created as one family,
may live together in tranquillity.

Collect

God and Father,
you teach us that those who make peace
shall be called your children.
Inspire your people everywhere
to seek and pursue that justice
which alone brings true and lasting peace.
We ask this through Jesus Christ,
our Saviour, now and for ever.

For those becoming Christians:

Let us pray for those preparing
to become members of Christ's Church;
that they may hear the word of God
and learn to put it into practice.

Collect

Gracious God,
you are the origin of every good resolve
and the fulfilment of every right desire.
Draw more closely to yourself
those who are learning to walk in the ways of Christ.
Guide them by the gospel,
and unite them in love and service
of you and their neighbour.
We ask this through Jesus Christ,
our Saviour, now and for ever.

For refugees, exiles and the persecuted:

Let us pray for all those
forced to flee their homeland,
and all who are persecuted
for their beliefs or way of life.

Collect

God of pity,
be moved by the plight of those
in exile from their native land,
and all who suffer at the hands of others.
Do not let them lose hope,
and strengthen the resolve of your people
to work for those whose need has stirred
the heart of your generous compassion.
We ask this in the name of Jesus,
our Saviour, now and for ever.

For reverence towards the earth:

Let us pray for reverence
towards the earth, our home,
that we may be good stewards
of all that the Creator entrusts to us.

Collect

Lord God,
by whose word the earth was made
and by whose hand it is sustained;
teach us to live in peace and respect
towards this earth, your bounteous gift,
so that in reverencing what you have given,
we may worship you, the Maker.
We make this prayer through Jesus,
our Saviour, now and for ever.

For the sick and suffering:

Let us pray for all who are sick,
that the Lord in mercy may help them,
save them and raise them up.

Collect

God, whose Only-Begotten Son
bore our sorrows and our weakness;
listen in mercy to our prayers for the sick,
that all who are burdened with pain or disease
may know that they are counted among those
whom Christ has named as blessed,
and that they are united to his sufferings
for the healing of the world.
We ask this through Jesus Christ,
our Saviour, now and for ever.

For all needs:

Finally, let us pray to God
for every human need,
that the loving Maker of all
may come to our help.

Collect

God, our help,
you have placed on our lips
the prayer of your Christ
for every need of humankind.
Give ear to this prayer, heed and answer
the cries of all people for peace and goodwill,
and in your compassion make us whole again
that we may respond in fullness to you
from whom we come and to whom we must return.

We make this prayer through Jesus Christ,
who is one with you and the Holy Spirit,
now and for ever.

Easter Eve – Holy Saturday

No formal liturgy (apart from Morning and Evening Prayer) is
required for Holy Saturday before the Great Vigil. Some good
collects do exist, however, in addition to the one in *Common
Worship* (p. 399) based on that in the *Book of Common Prayer*.

The Ambrosian collects translated below employ the ancient
image of 'The Harrowing of Hell' which is depicted in this ancient
Homily for Holy Saturday:

*A reading from an ancient homily 'For the Holy and Great
Sabbath'*

What is this? This silence over all the earth? What is this silence
and solitude? It is a great silence, for the King sleeps. The earth
was silent and afraid; for God sleeps in the flesh and raises from
slumber those who slept from ages past. God has died in the flesh
and Death is shaken.

Straightaway he goes to seek out our first parent, as a shepherd
searches for the lost sheep. He will visit those who sit in darkness
and the shadow of death: captive Adam, captive Eve. He will end
their grief, he who is God, and Adam's child.

The Master goes to them, holding the cross, the weapon of his
triumph. Adam, our first parent, sees him, beats his breast in awe
and cries out to all: 'My Lord be with you all.' And Christ in
reply says to Adam: 'And with your spirit.' Grasping him by the
hand he raises him, saying 'Awake, sleeper! Rise from the dead
and Christ shall be your light.'

'I am your God, who for your sake became your child. For you and your descendants I speak and command those who were in chains: Go forth! and those in darkness: Be light! and those who sleep: Awake!'

'I command you: Awake, you sleeper. I did not create you to be held in the fetters of death. Rise from the dead; I am the life of the dead. Rise, work of my hands; rise, my image, created in my likeness. Rise, let us go from here. For you in me and I in you, we are one person, one and undivided.'

Collect

O God,
you have searched the depths we cannot know,
and touched what we cannot bear to name;
may we so wait,
enclosed in your darkness,
that we are ready to encounter
the terror of the dawn,
with Jesus Christ,
Amen.

Collect

O God,
by whose will our Saviour
entrusted his body to the sleep of the tomb
and rescued from the rule of death
those who had been righteous in ages past;
grant that all who are buried with Christ in Baptism
may rise with him to freedom and new life,
and enter into that glory
where he is one with you and the Holy Spirit,
for ever and ever.

Collect

Christ, strong and gentle Saviour,
by the power of your sufferings
you have overcome the rule of death
and led the righteous of old
to the promised land they hoped for.
Grant new vigour to your Church,
that with free and joyful steps
it may tread the way
to the longed-for goal of your glory,
where you are one with the Father
in the unity of the Holy Spirit,
now and for ever.

Collect

Almighty and eternal God,
you ordained that in the death of Christ
the world should know
the darkness of abandonment;
we beg you,
flood your Church with the radiant light
of your Son, now risen from death,
so that without doubt or fear
your people may walk in the way of salvation.
Through Jesus Christ, our life
now and for ever.

The Vigil of Easter

The Easter Vigil should take place at night, starting after dark on Holy Saturday evening and concluding at dawn on Easter Sunday. Some churches celebrate an all-night vigil, where the Ministry of the Word is extended in different ways throughout the night, and the Eucharist celebrated at dawn. Other churches begin the vigil during the night or in the early hours of Sunday.

The Vigil is traditionally divided into four parts. First comes the Service of Light, in which the Easter Candle is lit from the New Fire, and carried into the church, where the Easter Blessing known as the 'Exsultet' is proclaimed.

The Ministry of the Word follows. The mighty works of God in creation and liberation of God's people are recalled.

The Service of Christian Initiation forms the third part of the Vigil. Adults who have reached the end of their Christian formation and instruction are baptized and confirmed.

Finally, the Easter Eucharist is celebrated.

The Service of Light

Outside the church a substantial fire should be prepared, round which the people gather. The ministers gather with the people. The president greets the congregation:

V/. The Lord be with you.
R/. And also with you.

The president or the deacon speaks to the people about the meaning of this Vigil, in words such as these:

Dear friends in Christ, on this night our Saviour Jesus Christ came forth from death into glorious life. On this night the Church gathers in vigil and prayer to celebrate the Passover of Christ. We keep the memory of Jesus, dying and risen, by listening to God's word and celebrating the sacraments. Through this joyful festival, we have confidence in the power of God, that we shall share in Christ's victory over death and become partakers in the resurrection.

Blessing of the Fire
Glorious God,
whose light has shone in all its fullness
through the resurrection of your Only-Begotten Son;

bless this new fire,
and fire your people with new hope
that the risen One will lead us
into the feast of your eternal light.
We ask this through Christ our Lord.

The Easter Candle is brought to the president.

The candle may be decorated, and among the symbols it bears might be a cross, with the digits of the current year inscribed around the cross, together with the Greek letters Alpha and Omega. The president may mark these symbols. If the candle is undecorated, the president cuts the symbols, speaking the words that follow:

Cutting or marking the vertical arm of the cross:
Christ, yesterday and today.

The horizontal arm of the cross:
the beginning and the end,

The Alpha:
Alpha,

The Omega:
and Omega;

The first digit of the current year in the upper left angle of the cross:
all time belongs to him,

The second digit in the upper right angle:
and all the ages.

The third digit in the lower left angle:
To Christ be the power and glory,

The fourth digit in the lower right angle:
for ever and ever, Amen.

Five grains of incense may be inserted into the candle. The president does this in the form of a cross, and says:

1 By his holy
2 and glorious wounds   1
3 may the Lord Jesus Christ   4 2 5
4 watch over us   3
5 and protect us. Amen.

The president lights the candle with a taper from the fire, saying:
May the light of Christ who rises in glory
scatter the darkness of heart and mind.

The president or the deacon lifts the candle high and sings:
Christ is our light.

All reply:
Thanks be to God.

The procession of ministers and congregation makes its way to the door of the church, where the acclamation and response is sung a second time, at a higher pitch than the first. A further station is made at the chancel step, where the acclamation and response is sung for a third time, again to a higher note.

The Candle is placed in its stand in a prominent position. The deacon, or whoever is to proclaim the Easter Blessing or Exsultet, places the text on a lectern. If incense is used, the candle, and then the congregation, is incensed.

Two versions of the Easter Blessing are given here. The first is an English version of the traditional text. The second is a modern composition.

The Easter Blessing (Exsultet)

Exult and sing, you angel choirs on high!
Rejoice, you powers of heaven and of earth!
Jesus Christ, the King, has triumphed!
Sound the trumpet! Ring out our salvation!

Exult and sing, O earth, in shining splendour,
radiant with the glory of your king!
You that once lay covered in darkness,
Now behold! Christ fills you with glory!

Exult, O Mother Church, with all your children,
splendid you stand in the risen Saviour's light!
Let this place echo your joy, O people!
Let these walls tremble with your shouts of praise!

V/. The Lord be with you.
R/. And also with you.
V/. Lift up your hearts.
R/. We lift them to the Lord.
V/. Let us give thanks to the Lord our God.
R/. It is right to give thanks and praise.

It is truly right and just,
that with full hearts and minds and voices,
we should praise you, God unseen, almighty Father,
through Jesus Christ, your Only-Begotten Son.

For Christ has shed his precious blood,
breaking the chains of Adam, our ancestor,
reconciling all men and women to their Creator.

This truly is our Passover feast,
when Christ the Lamb is slain
to hallow with his blood the homes of all his people.

This truly is the night,
when you delivered Israel from Egypt,
and led them dry-shod through the waters.

This truly is the night,
when you blazed like a fiery pillar,
and scattered the darkness of our separation.

This is the night,
when you rescue Christ's people from sin,
restore them to grace and unite them in holiness.

This is the night,
when Jesus Christ broke the bonds of death
and rose victorious from the dead.

For what had we to gain from living,
had we not known the blessing of redemption?

O God, how wonderful your kindness!
Your charity and love beyond all telling!
To ransom a slave, you yielded up your Son!

O sin of Adam, necessary sin,
which by the death of Christ is wiped away!

O happy fault,
which found so mighty a Redeemer!

O night of blessing, truly blessed,
chosen to know the time and the hour
when Christ arose from death!

This is the night, of which it is written:
'The night shall be radiant as the day;
the night shall be my light and joy!'

Holy is this night!
It dispels the works of evil,
washes guilt away, restores lost innocence
and brings joy to those in sorrow.
This holy night makes hatred flee away,
brings harmony to birth and humbles pride.

O night most truly blessed,
when heaven is one with earth
and humankind with God is reconciled!

Therefore, Father, on this night of grace,
receive the evening sacrifice of praise,
the solemn dedication of this candle,
the work of human hands, the labour of the honey-bee,
presented now before you by your holy Church.

For we have heard the praises
inspired by this fiery pillar,
kindled and brightly burning
before the glory of our God.

And though this fire divides in many parts,
its radiance knows no loss, it shines no less;
for it is fed by that same molten wax
created by the mother bee
to feed the flame of this most precious light.

Therefore, Lord, we make our prayer,
that this candle, consecrated in honour of your name,
may burn here bright and steady
to dispel the darkness of this night.
Let it be accepted, a sweet and perfumed gift,
and mingle with the lights of heaven.
May the star of morning behold its flame,
that star, that morning star which knows no setting:

Christ, your Son,
who came back from the dead
and shed his peaceful light on humankind,
Christ, who lives and reigns for ever and ever.

R/. Amen.

Another version of the Exsultet

The minister begins:
Exult and sing, O shining angel choirs!
Exult and dance, bright stars and blazing suns!
The firstborn of creation, Jesus Christ,
is risen in radiant splendour from the dead!

Rejoice, O awesome night of our rebirth!
Rejoice, O mother moon that marks the months!
For from your fullness comes, at last, the Day
when sin is robbed of power and death is slain!

Awake, earth! Awaken, air and fire!
O children born of clay and water, come!
The one who made you rises like the sun
to scatter night and wipe your tears away.

Arise then, sleepers, Christ enlightens you!
Arise from doubt and sadness, sin and death.
With joyful hearts and spirits set afire
draw near to sing this Easter candle's praise!

V/. The Lord be with you.
R/. And also with you.
V/. Lift up your hearts.
R/. We lift them to the Lord.
V/. Let us give thanks to the Lord our God.
R/. It is right to give thanks and praise.

The Three Days of Easter

We praise you, God, for all your works of light!
We bless you for that burst of fire and flame
through which you first created all that is:
a living universe of soaring stars,
of space and spinning planets, surging seas
that cradle earth and rock against her breast.

R/. We praise you, God of everlasting light!

We praise you for light's beauty, motion, speed:
for eastern light that paints the morning sky;
for western light that slants upon our doors,
inviting us to praise you every night.

R/. We praise you, God of everlasting light!

We bless you for the light invisible:
the fire of faith, the Spirit's grace and truth,
the light that bonds the atom, stirs the heart,
and shines for ever on the face of Christ!

R/. We praise you, God of everlasting light!

Creator, in the joy of Easter eve,
accept our offering of this candle's light:
may all who see its glow and feel its warmth
be led to know your nature and your name.

R/. We praise you, God of everlasting light!

For, Father, it was your own light and love
that led your people Israel dry-shod
through foaming seas and brought them safe at last
to lands of milk and honey. In your love
you led them as a shining cloud by day
and as a flaming shaft of fire by night.

This is the night, most blessed of all nights,
when first you rescued people from the sea:
a sign of that new birth which was to come
in blood and water flowing from Christ's side!

R/. Now is Christ risen! We are raised with him!

This is the night, most blessed of all nights,
when your creating Spirit stirred again
to turn back chaos and renew the world,
redeeming it from hatred, sin and strife!

R/. Now is Christ risen! We are raised with him!

This is the night, most blessed of all nights,
when all the powers of heaven and earth were wed
and every hungry human heart was fed
by Christ our Lamb's own precious flesh and blood!

R/. Now is Christ risen! We are raised with him!

O night, more holy than all other nights,
your watchful eyes beheld, in wondrous awe,
the triumph of our Saviour over sin,
the rising of the Deathless One from death!

R/. Now is Christ risen! We are raised with him!

O night that gave us back what we had lost!
O night that made our sin a happy fault!
Beyond our deepest dreams this night, O God,
your hand reached out to raise us up in Christ.

R/. Now is Christ risen! We are raised with him!

O night of endless wonder, night of bliss,
when every living creature held its breath

and Christ robbed death and harrowed hopeless hell,
restoring life to all those in the tomb!

R/. Now is Christ risen! We are raised with him!

And so, our God, creator of all life,
with open hearts and hands we come to you:
anointed with the Spirit's pow'r, we bear
these precious glowing gifts of fire and flame.

We pray that when our night of watching ends,
the Morning Star who dawns and never sets,
our Saviour Jesus Christ, may find us all
united in one faith, one hope, one Lord.

For you, O Lord, are God, living and true:
all glory, praise and pow'r belong to you
with Jesus Christ, the One who conquered death,
and with the Spirit blest for evermore.

R/. Amen!

The congregation are seated. The president announces the beginning of the Vigil.

Dear friends, beloved in Christ,
our solemn vigil has begun.
Let us listen and attend
to the tale of those wonderful works,
by which a universe was created,
God's people delivered from slavery
and in the fullness of time
united in the life of Christ, the risen Saviour.
Let these be hours of watching,
and may the Holy Spirit keep us ready
to welcome the coming of the risen One.

The Ministry of the Word

The Common Worship *Lectionary proposes the following set of readings for the Vigil. Attached to each reading and its respon-sorial Psalm is a collect. After the Psalm has been sung, the con-gregation may stand. The president will say 'Let us pray.' A silence should be kept and then the collect recited. In this way a rhythm of reading, response and prayer will be maintained.*

Genesis 1:1 — 4:4a The Creation

Psalm 136

Collect

How marvellous are your works, O God!
Throughout the order and beauty of creation,
each day sings of your glory,
each night utters your praise.
Teach us now,
how much greater in wonder
is the new creation,
by which in the fullness of time
you gave us eternal life in Christ, your Son,
who is one with you and the Holy Spirit,
now and for ever.

Genesis 7:1–5, 11–18; 8:6–18; 9:8–13 Noah and the Ark of Salvation

Psalm 46

Collect

God of steadfast love,
in the waters of the deluge
you swept away the world's corruption,
and in the saving flood of Baptism
you give us a new beginning in holiness.

Keep us faithful to your covenant;
purify all that is corrupt in us;
make us live according to your justice
and pursue the things that make for peace.
We ask this through Jesus Christ our Lord.

Genesis 22:1–18 The Binding of Isaac

Psalm 16

Collect

God, Father of all believers,
you promised to Abraham
that as he had obeyed your voice
you would bless him with a multitude of descendants.
Now, through the Passover of Christ, your Son,
you fulfil that promise for the whole world.
Let us respond wholeheartedly to your call
and in the obedience of faith
accept gladly the new life of grace.
We ask this through Jesus Christ our Lord.

Exodus 14:10–31; 15:20–21 Deliverance at the Red Sea

The Song of Moses and Miriam, Exodus 15:16–18

Collect

God of wonders,
whose right hand parted the waters of the sea
and saved your people from their oppressor;
unlock for us the meaning of this marvel,
and grant that every nation
may come to share the faith and joy of Israel,
by coming to new birth in water and the Holy Spirit.
We ask this through Jesus Christ our Lord.

Isaiah 55:1–11 Grace is free and limitless

The Song of Isaiah, Isaiah 12:2–6

Collect

God, our hope,
you spoke these words of mystery,
as your prophets foretold
the wonders we celebrate tonight.
Draw us back to you, for you are merciful,
so that we may find in your abundance
the fulfilment of all our desire.
We ask this through Jesus Christ our Lord.

Baruch 3:9–15, 32—4:4 A call for the people to turn again
or
Proverbs 8:1–8, 19–21; 9:4b–6 Wisdom speaks her praises

Psalm 19

Collect

God, fountain of all being,
by wisdom you have created the universe
and surrounded us with wonders
both in the heavens and on earth.
Open our lips and give us words to glorify you,
that in praise we may taste your joy,
and be made wise in the ways of your peace.
We ask this through Jesus Christ, our Lord.

Ezekiel 36:24–28 The new and cleansing water

Psalm 42/43

Collect

God of the Covenant,
renew your people
by the gift of the Holy Spirit,

and gather us together in Christ
in whose heart and spirit we receive
the gift of your new and immortal life.
We ask this through Jesus Christ our Lord.

Ezekiel 37:1–14 The Valley of Dry Bones

Psalm 143

Collect

Over the chaos of our abandonment,
the dryness of exhausted hope,
breathe, O God,
the Spirit that makes us living beings,
the mighty wind of your creation.
Stand us on our feet
and name us as your own;
revive what is withered in us
and give strength to what is weak,
so that your people, as one great multitude,
may witness to your steadfastness and truth.
We ask this through Jesus Christ our Lord.

Zephaniah 3:14–20 The Presence of God

Psalm 98

Collect

God of light and vigour undying,
look with mercy on the whole Church,
that holy mystery and sacrament,
and in your eternal providence
bring to fullness the work of our redemption.
Let the whole world see and know
that what was fallen has been raised up,
that what was old is now made new,
and that all things are being restored to wholeness

through Christ himself,
from whom they had their origin,
who is alive, now and for ever.

If there are people to be baptized, this Collect may be used in place of the previous one:

Be present, O God,
in this great act of your love,
and send the Holy Spirit of adoption
on those who are to be born again
in the waters of Baptism.
Let the work performed by our ministry
be confirmed and perfected
by your glory and power.
We ask this through Jesus Christ our Lord.

The New Testament Reading, the Alleluia and the Gospel reading conclude the Ministry of the Word.

Acclamations

V/. Alleluia! Alleluia! Alleluia!
R/. Alleluia! Alleluia! Alleluia!

Year A: Matthew 28:6
V/. The angel said to the women
'Do not be afraid, Jesus, whom you seek, is not here,
for he has been raised, as he said.'

Year B: Mark 16:7
V/. The angel said to the women
'Tell his disciples and Peter,
that he goes before you into Galilee.'

Year C: Luke 24:5
V/. The angel said to the women
'Why seek the living among the dead?
He is not here, he is risen.'

R/. Alleluia! Alleluia! Alleluia!

The Liturgy of Baptism

The Service of Baptism takes place here, as set out in Common
Worship *pp. 352ff.*

*If there are no candidates for Baptism, the congregation may be
invited to renew their baptismal promises. The president may
bless the water for sprinkling using the following prayer:*

Gracious God,
on this holy night we keep vigil in prayer,
recalling the wonder of our creation
and the wonder of our redemption in Christ.
You have made this night holy,
as the night of our deliverance.
We ask you then, to bless this water,
as we use it to remember the waters of Baptism
where we passed from death to life with Christ.
Renew in us the living fountain of your grace
that we may share the joy of those
who have been baptized this Easter.
We ask this through Christ our Lord.

Renewal of Baptismal Promises

*The congregation renews its faith in Christ, as in the Service of
Baptism in* Common Worship *p. 356.*

Sprinkling

An appropriate song is sung while the president sprinkles the people. The Orthodox Easter 'Troparion' hymn is suitable here. It may be sung to a version of its Russian melody:

Easter Hymn

Perhaps with verses from Psalm 68, to this tone:

The Intercession follows:

Almighty God,
who in the Passover of Christ
have begun the new creation;
grant to your whole Church
the gifts of joy and peace this Easter,
and by our celebration on this night,
prepare us for the feast of the age that is to come.
We ask this through Christ our Lord.

The Liturgy of the Sacrament completes the Easter Vigil.

Prayer over the Gifts

With joy, O God,
we prepare the table
of the Lord's Passover.

Joyful you have made us;
joyful now be pleased to keep us
unto the eternal life of your kingdom.
We ask this through Christ our Lord.

Eucharistic Preface

It is truly right and just, our duty and our salvation,
to sing your praise, Lord God, in every season,
but most of all to praise you on this most holy night
when Christ, our Passover, is sacrificed.

For Christ is the true Lamb
who took away the sins of the world,
who by dying has destroyed our death
and by rising has restored our life.

And so, in the joy of this Passover,
earth and heaven resound with gladness.
The angels and the powers of all creation
sing the ageless hymn of your glory: Holy . . .

Prayer after Communion

God of the Covenant,
you have nourished us
with the sacraments of Easter.
Fill us with your Holy Spirit
and unite us in your peace and love.
We ask this through Christ our Lord.

After the blessing, 'Alleluia' is added to the words of dismissal.

Easter Sunday of the Resurrection

Scripture-related opening prayer

Years ABC
God, our joy, our song and our salvation,
on this, the day that you have made,
you gather us to exult in the risen Christ.

Set our minds on the new life
to which Christ calls us;
fire our tongues with the words of witness
for which Christ has anointed us,
and thrill our hearts on this day of days
with the bread of truth
and the cup of the Holy Spirit.

We ask this through Jesus Christ,
our Passover and our peace
who is one with you and the Holy Spirit,
now and for ever.

Opening prayers

God our Father, creator of all,
today is the day of Easter joy.
This is the day on which the Lord
revealed himself to his disciples
and opened their eyes to what the scriptures said:
that first the Christ must suffer
and so enter into the glory of the resurrection.
May the risen One
breathe on our minds and open our eyes,
that we may know him in the breaking of bread
and follow him in his risen life,
for he is one with you and the Holy Spirit,
now and for ever.

or:

God of glory,
in the resurrection of Christ
you have conquered the power of death
and opened for us the way to eternal life.
Raise us up, renew us
on this, the greatest of all days,
so that by the working of your Holy Spirit
we may set our hearts on high,
to live eternally in Christ, the risen Lord,
who is one with you and the Holy Spirit,
now and for ever.

If a hymn before the Gospel is to be sung, the Easter Plainsong 'Victimae Paschali' (New English Hymnal 111) or 'Jesus Christ is risen today' (New English Hymnal 110) would be appropriate.

Acclamations

Years ABC
V/. The stone which the builders rejected
has become the chief cornerstone.

Years A and B: Matthew 28:7
V/. Christ is risen from the dead;
he goes before you into Galilee!

Year C: Luke 24:5b
V/. Why do you seek the living among the dead?
He is not here; he is risen!

Intercession

O God,
who in the resurrection of Christ
have made us a new creation,
grant that your people may persevere

in faith, hope and charity,
never doubting that you will fulfil
your promise of eternal life
in Jesus Christ, our Saviour
now and for ever.

Prayer over the Gifts

God, our praise and joy,
be present as we prepare the table
where your Church is nourished and reborn
through Jesus Christ, our Lord.

Eucharistic Preface

It is truly right and just, our duty and our salvation,
to sing your praise, Lord God, in every season,
but most of all to praise you on this most holy day
when Christ, our Passover, is sacrificed.

For Christ is the true Lamb
who took away the sins of the world;
who by dying has destroyed our death
and by rising has restored our life.

And so, in the joy of this Passover,
earth and heaven resound with gladness.
The angels and the powers of all creation
sing the ageless hymn of your glory: Holy . . .

or:

It is truly right and just, our joy and our salvation,
to give you thanks and praise, most gracious God,
fountain of all being, source of life.

Your Son Jesus Christ, though one with you in glory,
accepted death on a cross for our salvation.

This is the Passover foreshadowed long ago
in the sacrifice of Isaac, Abraham's beloved son,
and in the offering of a lamb without blemish
according to the tradition of Moses.
This is the Passover of Christ,
acclaimed by the prophets
as the One who was to bear the sins of all
and blot out their iniquity.
This day is our Passover feast,
resplendent in the blood of Christ,
a day of rejoicing, a season of gladness,
the day of new life for all your faithful people.

Here then let heaven resound with praise,
and earth re-echo its joyful song: Holy . . .

Prayer after Communion

God, our glory,
watch over your people
and bring us to the fullness of the resurrection
promised and foreshadowed by this Easter sacrament.
We ask this in the name of Jesus the Lord.

Easter Evening: The Conclusion of the Three Days of Easter

It is an ancient custom to celebrate a festal Evensong on Easter
Day. This differs from the usual Evensong in that it is celebrated
in procession. The procession, which should involve the whole
congregation, visits the baptismal font and returns to the altar.
This form of the service begins with the singing of Easter verses,
the lighting of the candles in the church and the hymn 'The table
of the Lamb is set' (a translation of the ancient Office Hymn for
Eastertide Vespers), which is best sung to the tune 'Gonfalon
Royal' (cf. *New English Hymnal* 128):

Verses:
V/. Christ the Lord is risen!
R/. Christ is risen indeed! Alleluia!
V/. Glory be to the Father, and to the Son;
and to the Holy Spirit:
R/. As it was in the beginning, is now and ever shall be;
world without end, Amen. Alleluia!

The Easter Candle, still burning after the Vigil and throughout the day, is used as the source for lighting all the candles in the church. This Song of Light may be sung:

Song of Light: Psalms 27, 139
V/. Alleluia! Alleluia! Alleluia!
R/. Alleluia! Alleluia! Alleluia!
V/. The Lord is my light and my salvation;
The Lord will make my darkness into light.
R/. Alleluia! Alleluia! Alleluia!

Hymn:
The Table of the Lamb is set,
The Lamb has clothed his guests in white;
Let us, whom through the sea he led
Ring out our joy to Christ, our Head,

Whose body given up for us
Upon the altar of the cross
Is now our bread, our cup his blood:
We live in him who lives to God.

On that first Paschal eve God spared
His people from the Angel's sword;
From Pharaoh's land he brought them forth,
From bitter bondage and from death.

Our Passover is Christ the Lord,
The Lamb once offered is our food;
Unleavened bread of truth he is
Who gave himself in sacrifice.

He is the perfect offering
Who broke for us death's fearful sting;
His folk from death and slavery
he leads to life and sets them free.

To Christ our Lord we now must pray
That his own joy be ours today;
When death shall come, grant Lord that we
May share your Paschal victory.

All praise to you, the Lamb once slain,
You died and now you live again;
Whom with the Father we adore
And Holy Spirit, evermore. Amen.

The Opening Prayer is said, which should be one of the Collects given above, pp. 128–9.

Then the procession to the font begins. Psalm 114 may be sung, with 'Alleluia' as the refrain for all to sing, or this refrain:

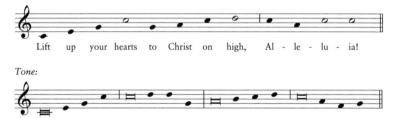

Lift up your hearts to Christ on high, Al - le - lu - ia!

Tone:

At the font, the first reading is Ephesians 1:3–14.

The Magnificat *is sung.*

The congregation may be sprinkled with water. If incense is used the font may be incensed. This prayer may be said:

Prayer
Father,
by your divine power
Jesus the Lord has risen in glory,
and with him, the people of the baptized
rise to new and eternal life.
Grant that your children
may know the greatness of your gift,
and inspired always by your grace
may be faithful to the baptismal covenant.
We ask this through Jesus Christ, our Lord.

The procession completes the circuit of the church and stops at the entrance to the chancel or sanctuary.

For this part of the procession, Psalm 116:1–8 is sung, with 'Alleluia' as the refrain, or this refrain:

The Lord has de - li - vered his peo - ple, Al - le - lu - ia! Al - le - lu - ia!

Tone:

When the procession reaches the chancel step, the congregation may be invited to return to their seats. The Second Reading is read, which may be either one of the Gospel readings for Easter Day, or the extract from Saint Augustine's Commentary on Psalm 148 given in Celebrating the Seasons *p. 230.*

The Canticle of Simeon, Nunc Dimittis, is sung.

The Three Days of Easter

A short homily may be delivered.

After the homily, the prayers of intercession are offered:

Intercession

Officiant: Christ is risen, and lives for ever to intercede for us.
With Easter joy let us complete our evening prayer:

Congregation: Ky - ri - e   el - ei - son!

Cantor: Pour out the Holy Spirit on your Church;
make it the sacrament of unity for all:
Congregation: Kyrie eleison!

Cantor: Lead all nations in the way of justice and peace;
that the earth may be filled with your glory:
Congregation: Kyrie eleison!

Cantor: You bore our weakness and carried our sorrows;
heal all sickness of body and spirit:
Congregation: Kyrie eleison!

Cantor: Overcome the powers that oppress your world;
let the poor and needy bless your name:
Congregation: Kyrie eleison!

*Additional intentions, names and commemorations may be
included here.*

Cantor: By dying you destroyed our death;
grant resurrection to the faithful departed:
Congregation: Kyrie eleison!

Officiant: Remember us, Lord, in your kingdom,
and teach us to pray: Our Father . . .

One of the Collects for Easter Day is said, or this Collect:

Today, O God,
the joy of Christ's resurrection
has spread throughout the world.
May his risen presence
remain amongst us and fill our hearts;
may his peace be with us and make us free,
until the coming of that eternal day
when we enter with Christ
into the glory of your kingdom,
where he lives and reigns
for ever and ever.

The Blessing
May God bless you on this day of days,
and shed his light upon you:
R/. Amen.

In the risen Christ God has healed us;
may he fulfil for you his promise of eternal life:
R/. Amen.

As you celebrate Christ's resurrection,
may you come to the feast that lasts for ever:
R/. Amen.

And may the blessing of God almighty,
the Father, the Son and the Holy Spirit,
be with you and remain with you for ever:
R/. Amen.

V/. Go, in the peace of Christ, Alleluia! Alleluia!
R/. Thanks be to God, Alleluia! Alleluia!

PART FOUR

PROPER TEXTS FOR THE SUNDAYS OF EASTER

For Easter Sunday see The Three Days of Easter, p. 128.

The Second Sunday of Easter (Low Sunday)

Scripture-related opening prayers

Year A
Blessed are you,
God and Father of our Lord Jesus Christ,
for the new birth which you have given us
in the resurrection of your Son.

We seek your blessing,
so that even though we have not seen,
we may be joyful in Christ our hope;
and though we have not touched the risen One,
let us know the Lord
as members of the body know their head,
for in glorious and undying life,
he is one with you and the Holy Spirit,
now and for ever.

Year B
By many signs, O God,
you have shown the glory of your Christ,
so that we may have life
through believing in his name.

Let that faith be exercised
in fellowship with the needy,
and be completed
in the joy and peace of the risen Jesus,
for in glorious and undying life,
he is one with you and the Holy Spirit,
now and for ever.

Year C
God, our salvation,
you have created this day for joy
in the One you have exalted
as firstborn from the dead.

Throughout these days of Easter,
open the hearts of your people
to the Holy Spirit he has breathed upon us,
and send us out to make known
the forgiveness and peace
we have received in Jesus,
for in glorious and undying life,
he is one with you and the Holy Spirit,
now and for ever.

Opening prayers

God of abiding mercy,
each year, as the feast of Easter returns
you kindle the fire of faith among your people.
Make us understand more deeply
the baptism of Christ, in which we have been washed,
the Spirit of Christ, through which we are reborn
and the blood of Christ, by which we are redeemed.
We ask this in his name, our Saviour,
now and for ever.

or:

God of terror and joy,
you arise to shake the earth.
Open our graves
and give us back the past;
so that all that has been buried
may be freed and forgiven,
and our lives may return to you
through the risen Christ, Amen.

Acclamation

Years ABC: John 20:19
V/. Alleluia, Alleluia, Alleluia.
R/. Alleluia, Alleluia, Alleluia.
V/. Jesus came and stood among the disciples
and said to them 'Peace be with you.'
R/. Alleluia, Alleluia, Alleluia.

Intercession

God of unity,
you have gathered a multitude of peoples
to acknowledge your name.
Grant that all who are reborn in baptism
may be united in one faith
and be of one mind in love.
We ask this through Jesus Christ our Lord.

Prayer over the Gifts

God of new life,
you accept the sacrifice of thanksgiving
from the lips of those reborn in baptism.
Let this sacrifice lead us to communion in Christ,
in whom is our eternal blessing.
We ask this through Christ our Lord.

Eucharistic Preface

It is truly right and just,
our duty and our salvation,
to praise you, Lord God, in every season,
but most of all in these most holy days
when Christ, our Passover, is sacrificed.

This is the day when your eternal Son,
who is one with you in glory,
arose as firstborn from among the dead,
to promise glory for that human body
in which he is one with us.

And so, in the joy of this Passover,
earth and heaven resound with gladness.
The angels and the powers of all creation
sing the ageless hymn of your glory: Holy . . .

Prayer after Communion

Eternal God,
let the Easter sacrament we have received
abide in us to touch our hearts
with the fullness of your saving grace.
We ask this through Christ our Lord.

The Third Sunday of Easter

Scripture-related opening prayers

Year A
God of glory,
by the Spirit of the risen Christ
you gather us together;
for Christ is the one who walks with us,

who opens the scriptures
and breaks the bread of life.

By your gift, we recognize him here;
make our hearts burn
to go back to the world
and speak your word of life in his name,
for in radiant glory
he is one with you and the Holy Spirit,
now and for ever.

Year B
God of mystery,
in a human body you showed the disciples
the marks of the crucified and living One.

Challenge us to respond to Christ
in the bodies of all who suffer,
so that the wounds which bring us healing
may be for the peace and salvation of all.

We ask this through Jesus Christ,
who in glorious and undying life
is one with you and the Holy Spirit,
now and for ever.

Year C
God of angels,
of living creatures and elders,
you are glorified in the many different gifts
displayed by your saints.

Let your praises in heaven be echoed on earth
in the worship and ministry of your people,
so that your Church may flourish in diversity
and be strong in the unity of your Spirit.

We ask this through Jesus Christ,
who in radiant and undying life
is one with you and the Holy Spirit,
now and for ever.

Opening prayer

God, whose unfailing stream of life
renews the strength and vigour of youth,
make us rejoice to be your adopted children in Christ,
and inspire us with the hope of a joyous resurrection.
We ask this through Christ our Lord.

Acclamations

Year A: Luke 24:31, 35
V/. Their eyes were opened and they recognized the Lord
in the breaking of the bread.

Year B: Luke 24:36
V/. Jesus himself stood among the disciples
and said to them 'Peace be with you.'

Year C: John 21:14
V/. This was now the third time that Jesus appeared to the disciples
after he was raised from the dead.

Intercession

God of our redemption,
look kindly on your Church.
Give true freedom to all who follow Christ
and lead them to the inheritance that lasts for ever.
We ask this through Jesus Christ our Lord.

Prayer over the Gifts

Gracious God,
with gladness we have prepared your table.
Grant, we pray you,
that as you give us cause for such rejoicing,
so you will bestow its fullness in eternal life.
We ask this through Christ our Lord.

Eucharistic Preface

It is truly right and just,
our duty and our salvation,
to praise you, Lord God, in every season,
but most of all in these most holy days
when Christ, our Passover, is sacrificed.

Through Christ the children of light
rise to eternal life,
and the gate of heaven's kingdom
is opened to your people.
For by his death we are set free from death,
and in his rising, life springs up for all.

And so, in the joy of this Passover,
earth and heaven resound with gladness.
The angels and the powers of all creation
sing the ageless hymn of your glory: Holy . . .

Prayer after Communion

Gracious God,
in the wonder of Easter
you begin your new creation.
Let this sacrament lead us
to the resurrection of the body
in glory that will never fade.
We ask this through Christ our Lord.

The Fourth Sunday of Easter

Scripture-related opening prayers

Year A
God, whose desire it is
that all men and women
should be drawn into one fold in Christ;

keep your people faithful
to the teaching of the Apostles,
the breaking of bread and the prayers,
so that among the conflicting voices of this world
we may hold fast to that of Jesus
and follow him before all else.

We ask this in his name,
for in glorious and undying life,
he is one with you and the Holy Spirit,
now and for ever.

Year B
God, our shepherd,
you make known the power of Jesus
wherever goodness and mercy spread your table
and compassion heals the sick and suffering.

Gather all your scattered children into one fold,
so that in love of one another, they may receive
the rich anointing of gladness in Christ,
who in undying life
is one with you and the Holy Spirit,
now and for ever.

Year C
God of glory and wisdom,
you give eternal life
to those who are faithful in following your Son.

Sustain us as disciples of Christ
and guide us in the paths of righteousness.
Bring us at last to your dwelling,
where there is no more hunger or thirst
and where every tear will be wiped away.

We ask this in the name of Jesus,
who in joyous and eternal life
is one with you and the Holy Spirit,
now and for ever.

Opening prayer

God of angels and saints,
lead us into the joyful fellowship
of those who sing your praise in heaven,
so that your little flock
may find its true home
where Christ our great Shepherd
has gone before us.
We ask this through Jesus Christ our Lord.

Acclamations

Year A: John 10:9
V/. 'I am the gate,' says the Lord;
'whoever enters by me will be saved.'

Year B: John 10:11
V/. 'I am the good shepherd,' says the Lord;
'the good shepherd lays down his life for the sheep.'

Year C: John 10:27, 29
V/. 'The sheep that belong to me shall listen to me,' says the Lord;
'no one will take them from my hand.'

Intercession

God, life of believers
and glory of the just,
listen in your kindness
to the prayers of your Church,
that those who cry to you in their need
may be sustained and consoled
with the abundance of your blessings.
We ask this through Christ our Lord.

Prayer over the Gifts

Make us joyful, O God,
in the fellowship of your table,
that the work of Christ
may continue among us
as the source of all our joy.
We ask this through Christ our Lord.

Eucharistic Preface

It is truly right and just,
our duty and our salvation,
to praise you, Lord God, in every season,
but most of all in these most holy days
when Christ, our Passover, is sacrificed.

By giving himself for our redemption
Christ abolished the sacrifices of old,
and he who is at once both priest and lamb
revealed himself as the perfect sacrifice.

And so, in the joy of this Passover,
earth and heaven resound with gladness.
The angels and the powers of all creation
sing the ageless hymn of your glory: Holy . . .

Prayer after Communion

God of every blessing,
enrich our minds and hearts
through this great feast of your love,
and as you have guided us into the way of salvation,
so make us worthy to reach its glorious ending.
We ask this through Christ our Lord.

The Fifth Sunday of Easter

Scripture-related opening prayers

Year A
God of all truth,
whose face we behold in Jesus,
build us as living stones
in a house of faith and communion,
founded on Christ, the cornerstone.

Let the good works
which you have prepared for us
be done for your glory in Christ,
who in eternal and undying life
is one with you and the Holy Spirit,
now and for ever.

Year B
Christ, our true vine,
let your word cut out from us
the deadness of indifference
and the corruption of untruth,
so that abiding in love
we may bear much fruit
and face your judgement without fear,
for in life that is eternal and bounteous

you are one with the Father and the Holy Spirit,
now and for ever.

Year C
God, whose promise
is a new heaven and a new earth,
secure and make strong among us
the new commandment of love;
so that the world may know us
as true disciples of Christ,
and be eager to join our pilgrimage
towards the eternal Jerusalem.

We ask this through Jesus Christ,
who in the fullness of life
is one with you and the Holy Spirit,
now and for ever.

Opening prayer

God, by whose gift
we are brought from separation
into fellowship with Christ;
be attentive to what you have wrought in us,
that those you have justified by faith
may never lack the courage
to endure all things with patience.
We ask this in the name of Jesus Christ our Lord.

Acclamations

Year A: John 14:6
V/. I am the way, the truth and the life,' says the Lord.
'No one comes to the Father except through me.'

Year B: John 15:1, 4
V/. 'I am the true vine,' says the Lord.
'Abide in me as I abide in you.'

Year C: John 13:34
V/. 'I give you a new commandment,' says the Lord,
'that you should love one another as I have loved you.'

Intercession

Hear the prayer of your Church, O God,
and fulfil the work you have begun
in the resurrection of your Christ;
so that through the gospel
your truth may be made known,
and through the witness of your people
the world may see your salvation.
We ask this through Jesus Christ our Lord.

Prayer over the Gifts

God, whose name we praise,
let our hearts be set on Christ,
and our lives be lived in thanksgiving
for all your blessings to us.
We ask this through Christ our Lord.

Eucharistic Preface

It is truly right and just,
our duty and our salvation,
to praise you, Lord God, in every season,
but most of all in these most holy days
when Christ, our Passover, is sacrificed.

In Christ, the world of the past is gone,
and the fullness of life is restored to us.

And so, in the joy of this Passover,
earth and heaven resound with gladness.
The angels and the powers of all creation
sing the ageless hymn of your glory: Holy . . .

Prayer after Communion

In your abiding love, O God,
be present to your people,
and as you have fed us with the gifts of heaven,
so make us pass into newness of life.
We ask this through Jesus Christ the Lord.

The Sixth Sunday of Easter

Scripture-related opening prayers

Year A
God unknown,
God revealed in Christ,
reveal yourself also
in the coming of the Spirit of truth.

Lead us into your house,
so that, with a clear conscience
and having a good hope,
we may practise your commandment of love
and face your judgement without fear.

We ask this through Jesus Christ,
who in blessed and undying life
is one with you and the Holy Spirit,
now and for ever.

Year B
By water and blood, O God,
and by the Spirit of truth,
you have revealed yourself in Christ
and formed the community of your Church.

Safeguard the unity of your people,
so that we whom Jesus calls friends
may keep his commandment of love.

For as he laid down his life for us,
so he now holds it in glorious fullness
with you and the Holy Spirit,
now and for ever.

Year C
God, our true home,
strengthen us in love,
and send the Advocate, the Holy Spirit,
to remind us of all your works and words,
so that through Christ
we may praise your glory
and walk joyfully in your presence;
for in light and radiance undimmed
he is one with you and the Holy Spirit,
now and for ever.

Opening prayer

Gracious God,
you have founded your people
on Christ, the precious cornerstone.
Let our daily living
rest securely on this foundation,
so that in the risen life of Jesus
our lives may find
the fullness of their meaning and their truth.
We ask this through Christ our Lord.

Acclamations

Year A: John 14:18
V/. 'I will not leave you orphaned,' says the Lord,
'I am coming to you.'

Year B: John 15:12
V/. 'This is my commandment,' says the Lord,
'that you love one another as I have loved you.'

Year C: John 14:23
V/. 'Those who love me will keep my word,' says the Lord,
'and my Father will love them, and we will come to them.'

or: Revelation 22:1
V/. The river that flows from the throne of God
is clear as crystal, the water of eternal life.

Intercession

God, our hope,
in Christ, the risen One
you walk with your Church,
unfolding your word
and breaking the bread of life.
Make us true witnesses to your tenderness,
and unite us as a community of welcome
for all who seek you.
We ask this through Jesus Christ our Lord.

Prayer over the Gifts

Let our prayers rise before you, O God,
as we prepare your table.
Purify us by your gracious presence
and fashion our lives
to be worthy of the praise we offer.
We ask this through Christ our Lord.

Eucharistic Preface

It is truly right and just,
our duty and our salvation,

to praise you, Lord God, in every season,
but most of all in these most holy days
when Christ, our Passover, is sacrificed.

Christ is our eternal priest,
who pleads our cause eternally before you;
Christ is the victim who dies no more,
the Lamb who lives as slain for ever.

And so, in the joy of this Passover,
earth and heaven resound with gladness.
The angels and the powers of all creation
sing the ageless hymn of your glory: Holy . . .

Prayer after Communion

Creator God,
who in the resurrection of Christ
have restored our life;
multiply in us the fruits of your saving work
and strengthen us in heart and body
with this food and drink from on high.
We ask this through Christ our Lord.

Ascension Day

Scripture-related opening prayer

Years ABC
On the clouds of heaven, O God,
a human being has passed into your glory
and our human nature is made one with you.

Set our hearts on Christ
and clothe our lives with power from on high,

that Christ may continue to work
through the witness and worship of your people,
until you bring that work to fullness
at his return in glory.

We ask this in the name of Jesus,
who is one with you and the Holy Spirit,
now and for ever.

Opening prayer

God of our gladness,
on this day we exult in thanksgiving and praise;
because the ascension of Christ
is our passage also into life,
and where the Head has gone before us to glory,
there we, the body, are called to set our hope.
We make this prayer through Christ our Lord.

Acclamation

Years ABC: Psalm 47:5
V/. God ascends with cries of joy;
the Lord goes up! The trumpet sounds!

Intercession

Gracious God,
gather your Church by the Holy Spirit,
that your people may be wholly dedicated
to your praise and glory.
We ask this through Christ our Lord.

Prayer over the Gifts

Let this table, O God,
stand for us at the gate of heaven,

so that we who offer
the sacrifice of thanksgiving
may share the joy of Christ in glory.
We ask this through Christ our Lord.

Eucharistic Preface

It is truly right and just, our joy and our salvation,
always and everywhere to give you thanks,
Lord, holy Father, almighty and eternal God:

For Jesus our Saviour, the King of glory,
triumphant over sin and death,
has ascended into the highest heaven
while angels gazed in wonder.
Christ, the mediator between God and humankind,
judge of all and ruler of the heavenly powers,
has not forsaken us,
but has given us the hope
that we, his members, shall follow him to heaven
where he, our Head, has gone before us.

And so, in the joy of Passover,
we sing the triumphant song of your glory: Holy . . .

Prayer after Communion

God, our hope,
you allow us while on earth
to handle things that are divine.
Let the affections of our Christian faith
be set on Christ,
in whom our humanity is made one with you.
We ask this in the name of Jesus Christ our Lord.

The Seventh Sunday of Easter

Scripture-related opening prayers

Year A
Living God,
you have given to your Son
the power of bestowing eternal life
on those you have entrusted to him.

Support and strengthen your people,
keep us alert in prayer and resistant to evil,
so that we may accomplish
all you give us to do in this world,
and rejoice before you
when your glory is revealed.

We ask this through Jesus Christ,
who is one with you and the Holy Spirit,
now and for ever.

Year B
All-wise God,
you know every human heart
and you protect the way of the just.

Sanctify us in that truth and unity
which is the gift of your Spirit,
so that we may abide in Christ
and bear untiring witness
to your victorious love.

We ask this in the name of Jesus,
who in eternal and glorious life
is one with you and the Holy Spirit,
now and for ever.

Year C
Christ, bright morning star,
raised and exalted in glory:
come, as you have promised.

Come, with the Father and the Holy Spirit,
and in that bond of mutual love,
make and keep us one.
Grant that we may abide in you,
and find our fulfilment in that threefold life
which was before the world was made,
and remains, for ever and ever.

Opening prayer

God of all creation,
we bless you for Jesus,
your servant and your Son:
for he stands before you on our behalf,
to intercede for all that you have made.
Raise us up to be one with Christ
in new and eternal life,
now and for ever.

Acclamation

Years ABC: John 14:18, 19
V/. 'I will not leave you orphaned,' says the Lord.
'Because I live, you also will live.'

Intercession

Look upon your people, O God,
gathered in prayer to await the gift of the Spirit,
and as we place our trust in your providence,
keep us faithful to your word of life.
We ask this through Christ our Lord.

Prayer over the Gifts

God of our praise,
let this act of service and fellowship
lead us into the glory of your presence,
together with Christ,
who is alive, now and for ever.

Eucharistic Preface

It is truly right and just,
our duty and our salvation,
to praise you, Lord God, in every season,
but most of all in these most holy days
when Christ, our Passover, is sacrificed.

Christ, the Lamb, his passion accomplished,
has ascended to your right hand,
and intercedes for us,
so that by the outpouring of the Holy Spirit
upon the waiting assembly of believers,
he may make us partakers of your divine life.

And so, in the joy of this Passover,
earth and heaven resound with gladness.
The angels and the powers of all creation
sing the ageless hymn of your glory: Holy . . .

Prayer after Communion

God of salvation,
through these holy gifts
maintain us in the sure hope
that you will fulfil for the whole body of the Church
what is already accomplished in the glory of Christ, its head,
who is alive, now and for ever.

The Day of Pentecost – Whit Sunday

The Greek title of this festival means 'the fiftieth day'. It is the last day of the Easter Season, which itself forms a sacred 'week of weeks' of forty-nine days plus one. Therefore Pentecost has been seen as the 'completion' of the Christian Passover observance. In the Jewish tradition Pentecost also 'completed' Passover, as a feast of the giving of the Law on Sinai.

Christian understanding united these ideas in the narrative of the gift of the Spirit by the risen Christ, to write the Law of God upon the heart of God's people.

Pentecost is, therefore, not a festival separated from Easter. It is the 'last and greatest day of the Festival' (cf. John 8:37) and its associations with water and the Spirit echo the baptismal themes of Easter. Pentecost is also a day for the baptism of adults.

Today the Easter Candle that was lit at the Easter Vigil is lit at the Eucharist for the last time, before being taken for the rest of the year to stand by the font in the place of baptism.

The prayers given below include some that are appropriate to a service where there are candidates to be baptized. See the suggestions for a Pentecost Vigil Service on pp. 244–50.

Scripture-related opening prayers

Year A
God of glory,
on this day you sent the Holy Spirit
to glorify the Christ whom you had sent.

Let your Church now rejoice
in the many gifts of the Spirit,
and empower us to use them
in speaking of your wonderful works
and exalting the name of Jesus.

We ask this through Jesus Christ,
in whom is our salvation,
now and for ever.

Year B
God of truth,
you sent the Holy Spirit
as wind and fire
to disturb and confound
the wisdom of our age.

Let the Spirit empower us
with words to challenge sin,
lives to express your justice
and confidence to announce
the coming of your judgement.

We ask this in the name of Jesus Christ
who in the new life of the Spirit
is one with you, God, now and for ever.

Year C
God, who on this day of wonders
sent among us the Advocate,
the Spirit of truth;
set us on fire with the gospel of Jesus
and give us boldness to announce
the mighty works which you have wrought.

We ask this in the name of Christ,
who in the new life of the Spirit
is one with you, God, now and for ever.

Opening prayers

Almighty God,
you have given us this holy season of fifty days
to celebrate the new life which is ours
in the Spirit of the risen Christ.
Let the Spirit gather the diversity of nations and tongues
and make them one body

to praise your glorious name.
We ask this through Jesus Christ our Lord.

or:

Almighty God,
you call us together to celebrate this feast,
and you sanctify your Church
in every people, nation and language.
Pour out the gifts of the Spirit
throughout the length and breadth of the earth,
and as your gracious love brought to pass
the first proclamation of the good news,
so now let that gospel be everywhere announced
through the work of those who believe.
We ask this through Jesus Christ our Lord.

or:

Spirit of truth
whom the world can never grasp,
touch our hearts
with the shock of your coming;
fill us with desire
for your disturbing peace;
and fire us with longing
to speak your uncontainable word
through Jesus Christ. Amen.

*Before the Gospel Acclamation, a suitable hymn may be sung,
such as 'Come, thou Holy Spirit, come' (*New English Hymnal
139).

Acclamation

Years ABC: Acts 2:4, 11
V/. They were all filled with the Holy Spirit,
and spoke in every language the mighty works of God.

Intercession

God of wonders,
by your Spirit of freedom
you transformed the apostles.
By your gift, they boldly announced your kingdom
and took up their mission with joy.
Visit your Church at prayer this day
and let the Holy Spirit breathe confidence
into all who are followers of Jesus.
We ask this in his name,
our Lord, now and for ever.

Prayer over the Gifts

Bless this table, Lord,
by the coming of your Spirit,
so that the promise of Christ may be fulfilled
and we may be led into all truth.
We ask this through Christ our Lord.

Eucharistic Preface

It is truly right and just, our duty and our salvation,
always and everywhere to give you thanks,
Lord, holy Father, almighty and eternal God.

Today you bestowed the gifts of the Holy Spirit
on your adopted sons and daughters,
and so you brought the feast of Easter to completion.
You sent forth the Spirit
as your first gift to those who believe,
to accomplish the work of Christ
and fill with your glory the whole of creation.

And so, in the joy of this Passover,
earth and heaven resound with gladness;
the angels and the powers of all creation
sing the ageless hymn of your glory: Holy . . .

or:

It is truly right and just, our duty and our salvation,
to celebrate the joy of this most holy day,
which in its sacred numbering of fifty days
reveals the fullness of the Paschal Mystery.

Today the confusion of languages
which human pride had brought upon the world
is resolved by the gift of the Holy Spirit.
Today, hearing the sound come suddenly from heaven,
the apostles received the profession of one faith
and spoke in many tongues,
announcing the glory of Christ's resurrection
to all the nations of the earth.

And so, in the joy of this Passover,
earth and heaven resound with gladness;
the angels and the powers of all creation
sing the ageless hymn of your glory: Holy . . .

or:

It is truly right and just, our duty and our salvation,
to give you thanks and praise, O God,
as we celebrate the day of Pentecost.

In the first days of your Church
the Holy Spirit imparted to all peoples
the knowledge of your Godhead
and speech to announce your wonders.
Through many gifts that differ
the Spirit works a wonderful unity.
In the variety of what is bestowed
the Spirit imparts all things in wisdom:
indeed it is the selfsame Spirit
who creates many tongues to proclaim your word
and bestows the faith which binds them into one.

And so, in the joy of this Passover,
earth and heaven resound with gladness;
the angels and the powers of all creation
sing the ageless hymn of your glory: Holy . . .

Prayer after Communion

God most high,
who bestow the gifts of heaven
upon your exultant Church,
make the presence of your Spirit
flourish in vigour among us,
that this spiritual food and drink
may bring us to eternal redemption.
We ask this through Jesus Christ our Lord.

*As Pentecost is the feast that concludes the Easter Season, it
should not have an 'octave' or eight-day prolongation as other
major feasts do. However, where it is customary to celebrate the
gifts of the Spirit in Whitsun Week, the following prayers might
be used.*

Opening prayer

Eternal God,
whom we dare to invoke as our Father,
make perfect in our hearts
the spirit of adoption as your children,
so that we may be ready to enter
the inheritance you have promised.
We ask this through Christ our Lord.

or:

Lord, we pray that the Holy Spirit
may come and enlighten us,
to make us mindful of Christ

and obedient to the good news of your kingdom.
We ask this through Christ our Lord.

or:

God, who in the glory of Christ
and the light of the Spirit
opened for us the way of eternal life;
grant, we pray,
that as we share in so great a gift,
so by your grace
we may respond with deeper faith
and grow in commitment to your service.
We ask this through Christ our Lord.

Intercession

Gather your Church, O God,
through the coming of the Holy Spirit,
so that your people may be wholly dedicated
to the service of your praise.
We ask this through Christ our Lord.

or:

Gracious God,
let the Spirit of your creation
breathe your new life into your people,
making them living stones
in the house of your glory.
We ask this through Christ our Lord.

Prayer over the Gifts

As we prepare your table, O God,
keep alive our wonder at the coming of your Spirit
and light the fire of your love in our hearts.
We ask this through Christ our Lord.

Proper texts

The third of the prefaces for Pentecost may be used.

Prayer after Communion

God, our righteousness,
in this holy supper you invite us
to place our lives in the hands of Christ.
Let your Spirit make us able
to respond to his call and embrace the gospel.
We ask this through Christ our Lord.

PART FIVE

PROPER TEXTS FOR THE SEASON OF EASTER

The following texts of opening prayers, prayers over the gifts and prayers after Communion are appropriate for the weekdays of the Easter season.

For the opening prayers, a short conclusion is given. Longer conclusions may be added if desired.

A collection of Easter weekday prefaces is also given, reflecting the themes of the Easter season.

Easter Monday

Opening prayer

God, source of life,
each year at Easter you bring new offspring
to increase the family of your Church.
Keep your people steadfast in faith,
and let the gift of grace received in baptism
be fully lived out in all our lives.
We make this prayer through Jesus Christ our Lord.

or:

Eternal God,
who in the resurrection of Christ
have raised us up to everlasting life;
lift up our hearts to the Saviour
who sits in glory at your right hand,
so that he who for our sake suffered judgement

may come to us as a merciful judge.
We ask this in his name,
who is one with you and the Holy Spirit,
now and for ever.

Prayer over the Gifts

Accept, Lord,
the worship that your people bring today,
and as we have received new life
through the profession of your name in baptism,
so may we attain the blessings of eternal life.
We ask this through Christ our Lord.

Prayer after Communion

God of blessings,
let the grace of the Easter sacrament
abound in our hearts and minds,
and as you have set our feet
on the way of eternal salvation,
make our lives worthy of your gifts.
We ask this through Christ our Lord.

Easter Tuesday

Opening prayer

Gracious God,
on this feast of Christ's glory,
you touch us with your healing power.
Raise up what is dead in us,
and support the new life you have given,
so that we may be truly free
to experience the joy of heaven
which even now we taste on earth.
We make this prayer through Jesus Christ our Lord.

or:

All-powerful God,
who in the blood of your Only-Begotten Son
have brought your people to freedom;
undo the fabrications of evil,
break the bonds of sin,
and as we have obtained eternal life
through the profession of your name,
let us live as those who no longer fear death.
We make this prayer through Jesus Christ our Lord.

Prayer over the Gifts

God of our joy,
let the table you prepare
bring us together in faith and hope,
so that the new life you have given
may lead us to eternal glory.
We ask this through Christ our Lord.

Prayer after Communion

God, who by water and the Spirit
have drawn us into your life of grace,
prepare your people for the eternal blessings
promised by these holy gifts.
We ask this through Christ our Lord.

Easter Wednesday

Opening prayer

God of wonders,
you transform despair into gladness
with the festival of Christ's resurrection.

Let the risen life of Jesus
be the source of our joy on earth,
and the pledge of eternal glory
for all who embrace his gospel.
We make this prayer through Jesus Christ our Lord.

or:

Christ, our life,
you came back to your disciples
in the glory of resurrection,
your passion accomplished.
Grant that we who celebrate your Passover
may know the consolation of your abiding presence,
now and for ever.

Prayer over the Gifts

God, at whose table
we offer the sacrifice of praise,
unite us in Christ, and accomplish in us
the salvation of mind and body.
We ask this through Christ our Lord.

Prayer after Communion

God, whose life is ever new,
in baptism you free us
from the oppression of sin.
Let the sharing of these holy gifts
renew us in Christ
and transform us into a new creation.
We ask this through Christ our Lord.

Easter Thursday

Opening prayer

Gracious God,
you have gathered together a diversity of peoples
in the acknowledgement of your name.
Let this people you have created
be distinguished by their unity in faith
and by steadfast love of you and their neighbour.
We make this prayer through Jesus Christ our Lord.

or:

God of truth and justice,
you have given us the Passover of salvation
in the Lamb who lives as one that has been slain;
set our hearts on Christ,
that our lives may give you praise
and all our works be done for your glory.
We make this prayer through Jesus Christ our Lord.

Prayer over the Gifts

God of community,
you gather those reborn in baptism
to dedicate your table with praise and thanksgiving.
Quicken now within your people
the desire to set their hearts on high with Christ,
who is alive, now and for ever.

Prayer after Communion

Listen to our prayers, O God,
and in sharing this sacrament
let us know your saving help
and be filled with the joy that abides for ever.
We ask this through Christ our Lord.

Easter Friday

Opening prayer

God, whose word is peace,
you have reconciled us to yourself
in the eternal covenant
which is the gift of the risen Christ.
Let your great joy be in us;
and as our voices give you praise,
so let our lives render you true and worthy service.
We make this prayer through Jesus Christ our Lord.

or:

God, our hope,
let the rising of Christ be for us
the pledge of a joy without end:
let it safeguard our dwelling in this present age
and fill us with longing for the age to come.
We make this prayer through Christ our Lord.

Prayer over the Gifts

God, at whose table
the gifts of creation become blessings from on high;
lift our hearts and minds to you,
so that our life on earth
may be filled with the joy of heaven.
We ask this through Christ our Lord.

Prayer after Communion

Eternal God,
watch over those you have saved,
so that as we are redeemed
by the suffering and death of your Son
so we may be joyful in his resurrection.
We ask this through Christ our Lord.

Easter Saturday

Opening prayer

God of abundant grace,
throughout the world you are increasing
the number of those who believe in you.
Look upon the people you call to serve you,
and as in baptism you give them new birth,
so clothe them with eternal life on high.
We make this prayer through Jesus Christ our Lord.

or:

God of wisdom,
you teach us by the Holy Spirit
to call on you as our Father.
Draw us more closely to yourself
in this bond and grace of adoption,
that we may know more fully
the joy of being your children.
We make this prayer through Jesus Christ our Lord.

Prayer over the Gifts

God of our praise,
let our thanksgiving come before you,
and may the new life of baptism
make us respond more deeply
to the continuing work of your love.
We ask this through Christ our Lord.

Prayer after Communion

God, our deliverer,
pour into our hearts
the strength of this saving feast,
that our lives may radiate the joy

of those you have set free to serve you.
We ask this through Christ our Lord.

The weekdays of Easter

After the second, fourth and sixth Sunday of Easter

Monday of the second, fourth and sixth week

Week 2: Opening prayer

God, high and exalted,
whom we dare to call our Father,
impart to us in fullness the spirit of adoption
whereby we are made your children,
and prepare us to enter
the inheritance you have promised.
We make this prayer through Jesus Christ our Lord.

Week 4: Opening prayer

God, our hope,
you raised up a fallen world
through the humility of Christ your Son.
Renew in us the joy of holiness,
and as you have rescued us from the slavery of sin,
let our unceasing delight be your praise.
We make this prayer through Jesus Christ our Lord.

Week 6: Opening prayer

Gracious and holy God,
let the Passover of Christ
be our source of joy in these days of Easter,
and bear abundant fruit for us in every season.
We make this prayer through Jesus Christ our Lord.

Prayer over the Gifts

God, our provider,
with gladness we have prepared your table.
Grant, we pray you,
that as you give us cause for such rejoicing,
so you will bestow its fullness in your kingdom.
We ask this through Christ our Lord.

Prayer after Communion

Loving God,
look kindly on your people,
and as you have made us your new creation,
lead us to the resurrection of our bodies
in glory that will never fade.
We ask this through Christ our Lord.

Tuesday of the second, fourth and sixth week

Week 2: Opening prayer

God, our joy,
enable us to proclaim
the good news of the risen Christ,
and as we acknowledge his resurrection
as the pledge of glory still to be revealed,
so make us partakers of the blessings it promises.
We make this prayer through Jesus Christ our Lord.

Week 4: Opening prayer

Gracious God,
let us who celebrate the resurrection of Christ
be open to receive the joy of our redemption.
We make this prayer through Jesus Christ our Lord.

Week 6: Opening prayer

God, whose unfailing stream of life
renews the strength and vigour of youth,
make us rejoice now
that we are your adopted children in Christ,
and inspire us with the vision
of the final resurrection
and the unbounded joy of your presence.
We make this prayer through Jesus Christ our Lord.

Prayer over the Gifts

God of our praise,
let our thanksgiving come before you,
and as you have given us new life in baptism,
so make us respond more deeply
to the continuing work of your love.
We ask this through Christ our Lord.

Prayer after Communion

Listen to our prayers, O God,
and in this exchange of gifts
let us know your saving help
and be filled with the joy that abides for ever.
We ask this through Christ our Lord.

Wednesday of the second, fourth and sixth week

Week 2: Opening prayer

God, Creator and Saviour,
year by year you make us recall
the dignity of our creation
and the glorious hope of resurrection.
Let what we celebrate once more in faith

become the pattern for our life in Christ.
We make this prayer through Jesus Christ our Lord.

Week 4: Opening prayer

O God, life of the faithful,
glory of the humble,
felicity of the just;
create in our hearts a longing for you,
that we may be filled with the sight of your glory.
We make this prayer through Jesus Christ our Lord.

Week 6: Opening prayer

Eternal God,
receive our prayer,
so that as we now celebrate
the resurrection of your beloved Son,
so we may be fit to rejoice with all the saints
when Christ returns in glory.
We make this prayer through Jesus Christ our Lord.

Prayer over the Gifts

At this table, O God,
you bring us into communion
with the richness of your divine being.
Let us, who have known your truth,
follow it worthily in the conduct of our lives.
We ask this through Christ our Lord.

Prayer after Communion

In your abiding love, O God,
be present to your people,
and as you have fed us with the gifts of heaven,
so make us pass into newness of life.
We ask this through Jesus Christ the Lord.

Thursday of the second, fourth and sixth week

(Thursday of the sixth week is Ascension Day, unless Ascension is celebrated on the seventh Sunday.)

Week 2: Opening prayer

All-merciful God,
let the Passover of Christ
be our source of joy in these days of Easter
and bear abundant fruit for us in every season.
We ask this through Jesus Christ our Lord.

Week 4: Opening prayer

God and Father of Jesus Christ,
you have raised our human nature
to share in your own divine bliss.
Continue the gracious work
which his resurrection has begun,
and fulfil the promise of glory in us
to whom you have given new life
through faith and baptism.
We make this prayer through Jesus Christ our Lord.

Week 6: Opening prayer

(when Ascension is celebrated on the seventh Sunday)
God, whose wisdom ordained
that our human being should be united
to your eternal Word,
and drawn thereby
into your story of salvation;
grant that we may so live as befits those
who are to inherit the joy of resurrection.
We make this prayer through Jesus Christ our Lord.

Prayer over the Gifts

Let our prayers rise before you, O God,
as we prepare your table.
Purify us by your gracious presence
and make our lives worthy
of the praise you give us to offer.
We ask this through Christ our Lord.

Prayer after Communion

Creator God,
who in the resurrection of Christ have restored our life;
multiply in us the fruits of your saving work
and strengthen us in heart and body
with this food and drink from on high.
We ask this through Christ our Lord.

Friday of the second, fourth and sixth week

Week 2: Opening prayer

God, who chose that your Son
should undergo the yoke of the cross
to drive out the enemy's power from our midst,
grant that we may be partakers
in Christ's resurrection and glorious life.
We make this prayer through Jesus Christ our Lord.

Week 4: Opening prayer

God of our freedom and salvation,
listen to the voice of those who cry to you,
so that those you have redeemed
through the blood of Christ
may know the joy of the resurrection.
We make this prayer through Jesus Christ our Lord.

Week 6: Opening prayer

(when Ascension is celebrated on the Thursday of this week)
God, our creator,
through the resurrection of your Son
you fashion us anew for an eternal destiny.
Encourage and strengthen our life in Christ,
so that when the Saviour returns in glory
you may clothe with immortality
those whom you bring to new birth in baptism.
We make this prayer through Jesus Christ our Lord.

(when Ascension is celebrated on the seventh Sunday)
God of truth, whose holy word
proclaims your salvation to the ends of the earth;
hallow your people anew
through the work of the risen One,
that we may enter more fully
into the life of your adopted sons and daughters.
We make this prayer through Jesus Christ our Lord.

Prayer over the Gifts

God of our joy,
let the table you prepare
bring us together in faith and hope,
so that the new life you have given
may lead us to eternal glory.
We ask this through Christ our Lord.

Prayer after Communion

Eternal God,
watch over those you have saved,
so that as we are redeemed
by the suffering and death of your Son
so we may be joyful in his resurrection.
We ask this through Christ our Lord.

Saturday of the second, fourth and sixth week

Week 2: Opening prayer

God, our Redeemer,
from you has come the spirit of adoption,
and in that spirit we cry to you as our Father.
Give us the freedom of your sons and daughters
and make us ready to receive
the inheritance that lasts for ever.
We make this prayer through Jesus Christ our Lord.

or:

God of compassion,
you open wide the doors of your mercy
through the wonder of Easter.
Look kindly on us, we pray,
so that as we follow the ways
you have marked out for us,
we may never stray from the path of life.
We make this prayer through Jesus Christ our Lord.

Week 4: Opening prayer

God, our Saviour,
in baptism you give us
the new life of faith.
Raise us up with Christ,
make our lives bear the fruit of justice
and lead us to the joy of your eternal dwelling.
We make this prayer through Jesus Christ our Lord.

Week 6: Opening prayer

(when Ascension is celebrated on the seventh Sunday)
Shape our minds and hearts, O God,
through the practice of good works;
keep us faithful to our baptismal promise,

so that, buried with Christ in the saving waters,
we may live in the light of the resurrection.
We make this prayer through Jesus Christ our Lord.

(when Ascension is celebrated on the Thursday)
God of glory,
through your Son, at his ascension,
you promised the Holy Spirit to the apostles.
Pour out upon your Church
the blessing of that same Spirit,
and through this manifold gift
renew and sustain it
for the proclamation of your good news
and the announcement of your kingdom.
We make this prayer through Jesus Christ our Lord.

Prayer over the Gifts

Accept us, Lord, as guests at your table
and make us a living sacrifice to your glory.
We ask this through Christ our Lord.

Prayer after Communion

We pray you, Lord,
that as we have received these holy things
in memory of your Son as he commanded,
so this holy feast may cause us to grow in his love.
We ask this through Christ our Lord.

After the third, fifth and seventh Sundays of Easter

Monday of the third, fifth and seventh week

Week 3: Opening prayer

God, our light,
you show your truth to those who stray

so that they may return to the right path.
Give the spirit of discernment
to all who are enrolled
in the profession of the Christian religion,
that they may reject whatever is contrary to it
and follow whatever is worthy of its name.
We make this prayer through Jesus Christ our Lord.

Week 5: Opening prayer

God of truth,
by whose gift alone
we can truly serve you,
let your precepts be our treasure
and your promise be our one desire,
so that amid a changing and inconstant world
our hearts may be set on you,
the source of abiding joy.
We make this prayer through Jesus Christ our Lord.

Week 7: Opening prayer

Let the power of the Holy Spirit
come upon us, O God,
that we may have the strength
to set our hearts always on your will,
and to carry out your purpose
in the conduct of our lives.
We make this prayer through Jesus Christ our Lord.

Weeks 3 and 5: Prayer over the Gifts

Let our prayers rise before you, O God,
as we prepare your table.
Purify us by your gracious presence
and make our lives worthy
of the praise you give us to offer.
We ask this through Christ our Lord.

Week 7: *Prayer over the Gifts*

By your gift, O God,
we lift our hearts to Christ on high.
Let your Spirit come upon us
and make us an everlasting gift to you.
We ask this through Christ our Lord.

Weeks 3 and 5: *Prayer after Communion*

Creator God,
who in the resurrection of Christ
have restored our life;
multiply in us the fruits of your saving work
and strengthen us in heart and body
with this food and drink from on high.
We ask this through Christ our Lord.

Week 7: *Prayer after Communion*

In your abiding love, O God,
be present to your people,
and as you have fed us with the gifts of heaven,
so make us pass into newness of life.
We ask this through Jesus Christ the Lord.

Tuesday of the third, fifth and seventh week

Week 3: *Opening prayer*

God, our help,
you open the gate of your kingdom
to those reborn of water and the Holy Spirit.
Increase the grace you have bestowed,
so that those you have set free from sin
may never lack the blessings

your faithful love has promised.
We make this prayer through Jesus Christ our Lord.

Week 5: Opening prayer

God of the living,
by the resurrection of Christ
you restore your people to eternal life.
Give us constancy in faith and hope,
that we may never doubt your intent
to keep the promises which you have made.
We make this prayer through Jesus Christ our Lord.

Week 7: Opening prayer

God, whose sevenfold gift we await,
let the coming of the Holy Spirit
sanctify your Church,
and make your people a temple
fit for the dwelling of your glory.
We make this prayer through Jesus Christ our Lord.

Weeks 3 and 5: Prayer over the Gifts

Gracious God,
with gladness we have prepared your table.
Grant, we pray you,
that as you give us cause for such rejoicing,
so you will bestow its fullness in your kingdom.
We ask this through Christ our Lord.

Week 7: Prayer over the Gifts

God, whose table is in heaven,
let our worship here lead us
to the fellowship of your holy ones on high.
We ask this through Christ our Lord.

Weeks 3 and 5: Prayer after Communion

Gracious God,
look kindly on your people,
and as you have made us your new creation,
lead us to the resurrection of our bodies
in glory that will never fade.
We ask this through Christ our Lord.

Week 7: Prayer after Communion

We pray you, Lord,
that as we have received these holy things
in memory of your Son as he commanded,
so this holy feast may cause us to grow in his love.
We ask this through Christ our Lord.

Wednesday of the third, fifth and seventh week

Week 3: Opening prayer

Eternal God,
be present with your people,
and complete in us the good work you have begun.
You have bestowed the gift of faith on us;
bring us to the inheritance of glory
promised in the resurrection of Christ your Son,
who is alive, now and for ever.

Week 5: Opening prayer

God, lover of innocence,
guide our hearts to seek you alone,
so that those you have set free
from the darkness of unbelief
may never depart

from the light of your truth.
We make this prayer through Jesus Christ our Lord.

Week 7: Opening prayer

Merciful God,
gather your Church in the Holy Spirit,
that it may be wholly dedicated to you
and be united in mind and heart.
We make this prayer through Jesus Christ our Lord.

Weeks 3 and 5: Prayer over the Gifts

God of our praise,
let our thanksgiving come before you,
and as you have given us new life in baptism,
so make us respond more deeply
to the continuing work of your love.
We ask this through Christ our Lord.

Week 7: Prayer over the Gifts

Father,
in obedience to your Son
we come to share your table.
Let the feast he prepares for us
make us holy in mind and body.
We ask this through Christ our Lord.

Weeks 3 and 5: Prayer after Communion

Listen to our prayers, O God,
and in sharing this sacrament
let us know your saving help
and be filled with the joy that abides for ever.
We ask this through Christ our Lord.

Week 7: Prayer after Communion

God of blessings,
let our sharing in this sacrament
give grace upon grace to your people,
and make us ever more ready
to receive your inestimable gift.
We ask this through Christ our Lord.

Thursday of the third, fifth and seventh week

Week 3: Opening prayer

God, source of every blessing,
let these days of Easter bring us
the spiritual gifts of the risen Christ.
As you have led us out of darkness
into your own wonderful light,
so let us praise the wonders of your love
and make known your salvation to all.
We make this prayer through Jesus Christ our Lord.

Week 5: Opening prayer

God, by whose grace
we are no longer strangers
and in whose love we are made blessed,
remember what you have accomplished
and the gifts you have bestowed,
so that those you have justified by faith
may never lack the courage of patient endurance.
We make this prayer through Jesus Christ our Lord.

Week 7: Opening prayer

God of abundance,
let the Holy Spirit

flood our lives with your gifts,
so that with hearts made pure, we may become
a holy and pleasing sacrifice to you,
fashioned and formed by your holy will.
We make this prayer through Jesus Christ our Lord.

Weeks 3 and 5: Prayer over the Gifts

God, whose name we praise,
let our hearts be set on Christ,
and our lives be lived in thanksgiving
for all your blessings to us.
We ask this through Christ our Lord.

Week 7: Prayer over the Gifts

Accept us, Lord,
as guests at your table
and make us a living sacrifice to your glory.
We ask this through Christ our Lord.

Weeks 3 and 5: Prayer after Communion

In your abiding love, O God,
be present to your people,
and as you have fed us with the gifts of heaven,
so make us pass into newness of life.
We ask this through Jesus Christ the Lord.

Week 7: Prayer after Communion

Generous God,
let this holy feast
enlighten us with your truth
and make us new in your undying life.
We ask this through Christ our Lord.

Friday of the third, fifth and seventh week

Week 3: Opening prayer

Most loving God,
you have brought us to know
the grace of the Lord's resurrection.
Let us be filled with the gifts of the Spirit
and rise again to newness of life.
We make this prayer through Jesus Christ our Lord.

Week 5: Opening prayer

God, our wisdom,
fashion our lives
after the pattern of Christ's resurrection,
so that the joy of the Easter sacraments
may bring us to our eternal salvation.
We make this prayer through Jesus Christ our Lord.

Week 7: Opening prayer

God most high,
you have displayed your glory
in the risen and ascended Christ.
In him you have opened the way to eternal life.
Grant us the light of the Holy Spirit,
make us grow in love of you
and enable us to use the gifts of the Spirit
in steadfast faith and trustworthy service.
We make this prayer through Jesus Christ our Lord.

Weeks 3 and 5: Prayer over the Gifts

Accept us, Lord,
as guests at your table
and make us a living sacrifice to your glory.
We ask this through Christ our Lord.

Week 7: Prayer over the Gifts

God of compassion,
look upon your people,
and purify our hearts
by the coming of your Holy Spirit.
We ask this through Christ our Lord.

Weeks 3 and 5: Prayer after Communion

We pray you, Lord,
that as we have received these holy things
in memory of your Son as he commanded,
so this holy feast may cause us to grow in his love.
We ask this through Christ our Lord.

Week 7: Prayer after Communion

Gracious God,
Let the Eucharist be once again for us
the food of life and the sign of your forgiveness.
We ask this through Christ our Lord.

Saturday of the third, fifth and seventh week

Week 3: Opening prayer

God of the Covenant,
through the waters of baptism
you give new life to all who believe in you.
Let all who are reborn in Christ
be strong to reject the glamour of sin
and stay faithful to the gospel.
We make this prayer through Jesus Christ our Lord.

Week 5: Opening prayer

God, our hope,
you grace us with your kingdom
and bring us to a new birth in baptism.
Guide us in this new life,
and since you have made us capable of immortality,
bring us at last to the full sight of your glory.
We make this prayer through Jesus Christ our Lord.

Week 7 (morning): Opening prayer

Gracious God,
in this holy fifty days
we have celebrated the Passover of Christ.
Make us always hold fast to this mystery
and in the manner of our lives
let us show forth its effect.
We make this prayer through Jesus Christ our Lord.

Weeks 3 and 5: Prayer over the Gifts

God of our joy,
let the table you prepare
unite us in faith and hope,
so that the new life you have given
may lead us to eternal glory.
We ask this through Christ our Lord.

Week 7: Prayer over the Gifts

Lord,
may the coming of the Holy Spirit
prepare us to celebrate the Lord's supper,
for that same Holy Spirit
is the forgiveness of all our sins.
We ask this through Christ our Lord.

Weeks 3 and 5: Prayer after Communion

Eternal God,
watch over those you have saved,
so that as we are redeemed
by the suffering and death of your Son
so we may be joyful in his resurrection.
We ask this through Christ our Lord.

Week 7: Prayer after Communion

God, whose love makes all things new,
you called us forth from the baptismal waters
and sealed us with the Holy Spirit.
By this sacrament, make perfect in us
the gracious work you have begun.
We ask this through Christ our Lord.

Eucharistic Prefaces for Eastertide

New life in Christ

It is truly right and just
in this holy Passover season
to praise and thank you, God of new life,
through Christ, the risen Lord.

Because in Christ
the world of the past has gone
and life in its fullness is restored to us.

And so, with boundless joy
we are one with the angels as we sing: Holy . . .

Christ, freely laying down his life

We lift our hearts to you, our God,
and in the joy of this Passover
we praise and thank you
through Jesus Christ our Saviour.

These are the days when your eternal Son,
having power to lay down his life
and power to take it up again,
arose as firstborn among the dead
to glorify our flesh and spirit,
that same human nature he had united to himself.

And so, with boundless joy,
we are one with the angels as we sing: Holy . . .

The Passover into eternal life

It is truly right and just, our duty and our salvation,
to praise you, Lord, at all times,
but most of all in this most holy season
when Christ became our Passover sacrifice.

In the glory of Christ's resurrection
eternal life begins, glory is foreshadowed
and the source of joy is opened for all.

And so, with glad exultation,
we are one with the angels as we sing: Holy . . .

Christ overcomes death

We lift our hearts to you, our God,
and in the joy of this Passover
we praise and thank you
through Jesus Christ our Saviour.

The Season of Easter

In Christ the bitterness of death is overcome
and the fullness of life eternal is promised to his people.

The joy of the resurrection
brings new life to the world,
and the choirs of angels sing to your glory: Holy . . .

Christ, risen, ascended, glorified

It is truly right and just
in this holy Passover season
to praise and thank you, God of new life,
through Christ, the risen Lord.

In his triumph over sin and death
he remains as one of us and gives us hope
that where he, our head, has gone,
there we, the body, shall surely follow.

And so, with angels and all saints
we glorify your holy name: Holy . . .

Christ, giver of the Spirit, judge of the age to come

We lift our hearts to you, our God,
and in the joy of this Passover
we praise and thank you
through Jesus Christ our Saviour.

Enthroned at your right hand in glory,
Christ bears our human nature united to himself,
thus to bestow the Holy Spirit,
thus to return and do justice for the living and the dead.

And so, with glad exultation,
we are one with the angels as we sing: Holy . . .

PART SIX

PROPER TEXTS FOR THE FESTIVALS AND FEASTS DURING LENT AND EASTER TIME

Lent and Easter have fewer Saints' days than other times of the Christian Year. This is because they are seasons with a particular focus. Many churches celebrate the principal holy days and leave the lesser ones as optional. The texts given below are for those days that are regularly kept during Lent and Easter.

1 March Saint David

Saint David, about whom little is known, belonged to the monastic movement of the fifth and sixth centuries CE, *linked with Gaul and Ireland, which was so influential in the coming of the Christian faith to Wales. Many churches across South Wales claim David as their founder. His chief foundation was at Mynyw (Menevia) in the far west of Dyfed. David was canonized by Pope Callistus II in 1123. As David is a National Patron, a full set of texts is offered for this day.*

Scripture-related opening prayer

God most holy,
who gave to Saint David
the water of wisdom to drink,
open to us that same abundant fountain

that we may share his delight
in the lore and teaching of Christ.

We ask this in the name of Jesus
who is one with you and the Holy Spirit,
now and for ever.

Opening prayer

O God,
who gave your servant David
the virtue of wisdom and the gift of eloquence
and made him an example of prayer and pastoral zeal;
grant that your Church, the fruit of his teaching,
may ever prosper and give you joyful praise.
We ask this through Jesus Christ our Lord.

Acclamation

Psalm 67:3

V/. Let the peoples praise you, O God;
let all the peoples praise you.

Intercession

God our Father,
you gave the bishop David to the Welsh church
to uphold the faith
and to be an example of Christian perfection.
In this changing world, let his example help us
to hold fast the values that bring eternal life.
We ask this through Christ our Lord.

Prayer over the Gifts

Bring us, O God,
as joyful guests to your table,

and with the bread of your word
nourish in us that faith
which Saint David taught
by word and by example.
We ask this through Christ our Lord.

Eucharistic Preface

It is truly right and just, our joy and our salvation,
always and everywhere to give you thanks,
God all-holy, strong and eternal,
through Jesus Christ our Lord.

Christ willed his Church to be the sign of salvation
when he sent forth apostles to announce the good news
and make all nations disciples of his teaching.
With eager heart, Saint David followed their example
and through his ministry planted your Church
among our ancestors in this land,
to open for them the way of salvation
through the life-giving mystery of Christ.

And so, with angels and all saints
we exult and glorify your holy name: Holy . . .

Prayer after Communion

Almighty God,
grant that in the strength of this holy gift
we may follow Saint David
in seeking you above all things
and living the new life of Christ.
We ask this through Christ our Lord.

17 March Saint Patrick

Patrick was born in Roman Britain at the end of the fourth century. Abducted and taken to Ireland by raiders early in his life, he died in Ireland about the middle of the fifth century. As a missionary bishop in Ireland he faced hardship, even opposition from fellow Christians. He worked to bring peace between kingdoms and tribes, to educate and to establish monastic life, which became the backbone of the early Irish Church. His own auto-biography testifies to the simplicity of his faith and his fearless preaching of Christ's gospel. As a National Patron, he is included in this collection.

Scripture-related opening prayer

Bind your name upon us,
O God of threefold glory,
and as you chose Patrick before his birth
to be a prophet to the nations,
so equip us with the shield of faith
and the breastplate of justice,
to proclaim the gospel of your peace.

We make this prayer through Jesus Christ,
who is one with you and the Holy Spirit,
now and for ever.

Opening prayer

God, true Shepherd,
whose wise providence sent the bishop Patrick
to preach your glory to the people of Ireland,
let his example inspire your Church
to rejoice in the name of Christian
and to be the herald of your wonderful works.
We ask this through Jesus Christ our Lord.

Ministry of the Word

Old Testament Reading: Jeremiah 1:4–9

Psalm 67

New Testament Reading: Ephesians 6:10–17

Acclamation (Lenten form)

Luke 4:18

V/. Christ our Saviour, glory to you!
R/. Christ our Saviour, glory to you!
V/. God sent me to bring the good news to the poor,
and freedom to those in prison.
R/. Christ our Saviour, glory to you!

*If the Acclamation is used outside Lent, 'Alleluia' is said in place
of 'Christ our Saviour, glory to you!'*

Intercession

God of salvation,
by the preaching of Patrick your bishop
you summoned a nation to follow the gospel of Christ.
Let the words of eternal life make us grow
in faith and knowledge of your glory.
We ask this in the name of Jesus Christ our Lord.

Prayer over the Gifts

Greet us with your peace, O God,
as we gather at your table,
and in your mercy unite us
with the multitude who praise you in heaven.
We ask this through Christ our Lord.

Eucharistic Preface

It is truly right and just, our joy and our salvation,
always and everywhere to give you thanks,
Lord, holy Father, almighty and eternal God,
through Jesus Christ our Lord.

By your Holy Spirit you chose the bishop Patrick
to bring the light of your gospel
to peoples that did not know you.
You called him to be all things to everyone
as a minister of your word,
so that the nations might become
a holy sacrifice, acceptable in your sight.

And so, with angels and all saints,
we glorify your holy name: Holy . . .

Prayer after Communion

Holy God,
we honour you, glorious in your saints,
and we share the gifts of salvation.
Make us glad as we remember Saint Patrick,
and joyful in the faith we have received.
We ask this through Christ our Lord.

19 March Saint Joseph of Nazareth

*Saint Matthew's Gospel portrays Joseph as a descendant of the
Royal House of David, and as one to whom God communicates
in dreams, like Joseph, the Patriarch Jacob's son. His cult took
root in the Latin churches in the late Middle Ages.*

Proper texts

Scripture-related opening prayer

God of salvation,
you make known your mysterious purpose,
and you give us the faith to follow it.

We pray that like Saint Joseph
we may hear your calling, do your bidding
and welcome the coming of your Christ,
who is one with you and the Holy Spirit,
now and for ever.

Opening prayer

All-powerful God,
let Saint Joseph be an example for your Church,
so that your people may fulfil their vocation
to become the body of Christ your Son,
whom you entrusted to his faithful care.
We make this prayer through Jesus Christ our Lord.

Acclamation (Lenten form)

Matthew 1:20

V/. Christ our Saviour, glory to you!
R/. Christ our Saviour, glory to you!
V/. The Angel said: 'Joseph, son of David,
do not be afraid to take Mary home as your wife,
for the child conceived in her is from the Holy Spirit.'
R/. Christ our Saviour, glory to you!

*If the Acclamation is used outside Lent, 'Alleluia' is said in place
of 'Christ our Saviour, glory to you!'*

Intercession

Loving God,
keep your household

always under your protection,
that we may remain always faithful to you.
We ask this through Jesus Christ our Lord.

Prayer over the Gifts

Lord, as we come to your table,
strengthen our communion as your family
and our fellowship with all the saints.
We ask this through Christ our Lord.

Eucharistic Preface

We lift up our hearts to you,
God eternal, true and faithful;
to you we offer thanks and praise
through Jesus Christ your Son.

We honour Saint Joseph,
that righteous man, given by you as husband
to Mary, the virgin Mother of God.
We celebrate his wise and faithful stewardship,
his fatherly love which guarded your Son,
conceived by the Holy Spirit.

And so, with angels and saints,
we glorify your holy name: Holy . . .

Prayer after Communion

Lord God,
watch over your Church
and as you nourish us
with the bread of heaven
safeguard also the gifts
your grace has showered upon us.
We ask this through Christ our Lord.

25 March The Annunciation of the Lord

This feast celebrates the Incarnation of the Word. Once regard-
ed as a feast of the Blessed Virgin Mary, it is really a feast of
Christ, like Christmas with which it is intimately connected.
Mary's acceptance of God's will, which is both the initiative of
grace and her grace-filled response, symbolizes the union of the
two natures, divine and human, in the person of Christ.

Scripture-related opening prayer

Holy God,
you have made us holy
by the Incarnation of your Son,
conceived when Mary responded in faith
to the message of the angel.

As Jesus became obedient to your will,
so let his unique offering
consecrate for you a people
for ever dedicated to your purpose.

We ask this through Jesus Christ,
who is one with you and the Holy Spirit,
now and for ever.

Opening prayer

Eternal God,
you chose that your Word
should be incarnate in the womb of the Virgin Mary.
Grant that as we acknowledge Christ our Redeemer
to be truly God and truly human,
so we may become partakers of the divine nature.
We ask this through Jesus Christ our Lord.

Festivals and Feasts during Lent and Easter Time

Acclamation (Lenten form)

Luke 1:37

V/. Christ our Saviour, glory to you!
R/. Christ our Saviour, glory to you!
V/. Mary said: 'Here am I, the servant of the Lord;
let it be with me according to your word.'
R/. Christ our Saviour, glory to you!

If the Acclamation is used outside Lent, 'Alleluia' is said in place of 'Christ our Saviour, glory to you!'

Intercession

O unknown God,
whose presence is announced
not among the impressive
but in obscurity;
come, overshadow us now,
and speak to our hidden places;
that, entering your darkness with joy,
we may choose to co-operate with you,
through Jesus Christ, Amen.

Prayer over the Gifts

God, who by the Incarnation of your Son
gave to the Church its first beginning,
accept the sacrifice of praise
which we offer today
to celebrate the coming of the Word made flesh.
We ask this through Christ our Lord.

Eucharistic Preface

It is truly right and just, our duty and our salvation,
always and everywhere to give you thanks,

Lord, holy Father, almighty and eternal God,
through Jesus Christ our Lord.

The Virgin Mary listened in faith
to the message of your angel
that the Holy Spirit would overshadow her
and that she would bear a son for our salvation.
In her most pure womb she was to carry him,
so that your promise to the children of Israel
might in truth be fulfilled
and the hope of all the nations
be made real beyond all telling.

Through Christ the choirs of angels
worship for ever before your glory;
with them, we pray you, join our voices
in this, their hymn of joyful acclamation: Holy . . .

Prayer after Communion

Lord God,
we acknowledge the child born of the Virgin Mary
as truly your Son and truly one of us.
Let this faith be strong in our hearts
and through the power of Christ's resurrection
lead us to the joy of your eternal kingdom.
We ask this through Christ our Lord.

23 April Saint George

Saint George was martyred at Lydda in Palestine, probably during the reign of the Emperor Diocletian. Legend and iconography portray him as a soldier. He is a popular saint in the Eastern churches, and is acknowledged as the patron or protector saint of several nations including England. His cult is bound up with many aspects of English culture, both religious and secular.

Scripture-related opening prayer

God, our freedom,
you have trodden down the power of evil
through the death and resurrection of your Christ.

Strengthen the faith of your people
by the example of Saint George the martyr,
that, dying with Christ, we may also live with him
and, being faithful, we may enter his kingdom.

We ask this through Jesus Christ,
who is one with you and the Holy Spirit,
now and for ever.

Opening prayer

Almighty God,
whose servant George
followed in the footsteps of Christ
and shed his blood for the faith;
let his example come to our aid
and his strength be manifest in our weakness.
We ask this through Jesus Christ our Lord.

Acclamation

Psalm 126:6

V/. Alleluia! Alleluia! Alleluia!
R/. Alleluia! Alleluia! Alleluia!
V/. Those who sow in tears,
shall reap with songs of joy.
R/. Alleluia! Alleluia! Alleluia!

Intercession

God of blessing,
strengthen your people,

that they may avoid evil, shun temptation
and find in you the fulfilment of their desire.
We ask this through Jesus Christ our Lord.

Prayer over the Gifts

Lord God,
let your table be a place of grace and welcome for us,
that as we are united in the sacrifice of thanksgiving,
so we may share in the destiny of all your saints.
We ask this through Jesus Christ our Lord.

Eucharistic Preface

It is truly right and just,
our joy and our salvation,
always and everywhere to give you thanks,
Lord, holy Father, almighty and eternal God.

Your holy martyr George took strength from you
to undergo his death with courage,
and through the shedding of his blood
he became a true follower of Christ.
He left this world of transient light
for a blessed and eternal home,
there to receive the unfading crown
of light that shines for all eternity.

With angels and saints we adore you,
and glorify your holy name: Holy . . .

Prayer after Communion

Let this holy feast, Lord,
keep us in your love,
make us true witnesses to the resurrection
and bring us to eternal life.
We ask this through Jesus Christ our Lord.

25 April Saint Mark, Evangelist

Saint Mark is usually identified with the John Mark whose mother's house in Jerusalem was a meeting place for the apostles. He is also identified with the young man who fled the garden of Gethsemane after the arrest of Jesus. Tradition associates him particularly with Saint Peter, and the Gospel of Mark is by tradition held to reflect Peter's preaching. Mark is honoured as the founder of the church in Alexandria.

Scripture-related opening prayer

God, whose wisdom
is revealed in the cross of Christ;
hide within our hearts
the secret of your saving plan,
so that, when we have to speak,
your Holy Spirit will give us
all that we need to announce
the power and gentleness of your good news.

We make this prayer through Jesus Christ,
who is one with you and the Holy Spirit,
now and for ever.

Opening prayer

Gracious God,
you bestowed on Mark the evangelist
the task of recording the gospel of Jesus;
transform our lives by this teaching
that we may walk with trust and joy
in the way of Christ.
We ask this in his name,
our Saviour, now and for ever.

Proper texts

Acclamation

Psalm 119:12

V/. Alleluia! Alleluia! Alleluia!
R/. Alleluia! Alleluia! Alleluia!
V/. Blessed are you, O Lord;
teach me your statutes.
R/. Alleluia! Alleluia! Alleluia!

Intercession

Sustain your Church, Lord,
that your people may have the courage
to announce the glory of the Son of Man,
who is alive and reigns, now and for ever.

Prayer over the Gifts

Draw us, O God,
by your gospel
into the fellowship of thanksgiving
and the feast of salvation
which we find at your table.
We ask this through Jesus Christ our Lord.

Eucharistic Preface

It is truly right and just, our joy and our salvation,
always and everywhere to give you thanks,
Holy Father, eternal God,
through Jesus Christ your Son.

You established that the mystery of our salvation
should be made known through holy Scriptures,
the work of authors chosen and inspired
by the light of the Holy Spirit.
In this way the words and deeds of our Saviour,

written in the pages of the eternal Gospel,
have been entrusted to your Church
to become a fertile seed
which bears the fruit of grace and glory for ever.

And so, with angels and all saints,
we glorify your holy name: Holy . . .

Prayer after Communion

Holy God,
by the gifts we share at your altar
make us holy,
and establish us in the faith
proclaimed by your evangelist Saint Mark.
We ask this through Christ our Lord.

1 May Saints Philip and James, Apostles

*Philip was from Bethsaida in Galilee. He became a disciple of
Jesus and one of the Twelve. The Fourth Gospel records (John
1:45) that he acclaimed Jesus as the one foretold by Moses and
the prophets. According to the book of Acts (Acts 8:5) he was the
first to preach the gospel to non-Jews.*

*James, son of Alphaeus, was also one of those called by Jesus
(Mark 3:18). He is known traditionally as James 'the Less'.*

Scripture-related opening prayer

Gracious God,
you have made known to us
the mystery of your will
through the coming of Jesus, your Christ,
and the preaching of the Apostles.

As we celebrate Philip and James
let us experience the power of the risen Christ
and perform the works which he has given us,
so that you may be glorified in your Son,
who is one with you and the Holy Spirit,
now and for ever.

Opening prayer

Eternal God,
each year we honour the mission and the glory
of your apostles Philip and James.
Fill us with the Spirit that gave them courage
to proclaim the gospel of Christ your Son,
who is alive, and reigns with you and the Holy Spirit,
now and for ever.

Acclamation

John 14:13

V/. Alleluia! Alleluia! Alleluia!
R/. Alleluia! Alleluia! Alleluia!
V/. Jesus says: 'I will do
whatever you ask in my name.'
R/. Alleluia! Alleluia! Alleluia!

Intercession

Lord, let your Church always give you glory,
for you are our source of life
and in your will is our peace.
We ask this through Christ our Lord.

Prayer over the Gifts

Lord, open our lips to praise you,
so that our worship on this feast of your apostles

may be worthy of the glorious grace
that you have showered upon us.
We ask this through Christ our Lord.

Eucharistic Preface

It is truly right and just, our joy and our salvation,
always and everywhere to give you thanks,
Holy Father, eternal God,
through Jesus Christ your Son.

By your gracious call
Philip and James became disciples of Christ,
desiring to know you in fullness of truth.
Confirmed in faith by the resurrection of the Master,
they became his faithful witnesses,
steadfast even to death.
Now, in this assembly gathered for your glory,
we rejoice to share in that redemption
which their preaching has made known to us.

And so, with angels and all saints
we glorify your holy name: Holy . . .

Prayer after Communion

God, source of blessings,
let these holy gifts
work in our minds and hearts,
so that we may see you more clearly
in the face of Jesus Christ
and come to possess eternal life.
We ask this through Christ our Lord.

4 May English Saints and Martyrs of the Reformation Era

The English Reformation, which lasted for much of the mid six-teenth century, was a contentious political and religious upheaval, in the course of which many men and women were called upon to suffer for their beliefs. The Calendar of Common Worship *contains commemorations of martyrs from both sides of the divide.*

Scripture-related opening prayer

Faithful God,
you formed us for your glory.

Strengthen us by the witness of those
who accepted death for their faith,
so that in affliction we may not be crushed
nor driven to despair in perplexity,
but as we bear in our body the death of Jesus,
so also show forth in us his victorious life.

We ask this in the name of Jesus,
who is one with you and the Holy Spirit,
now and for ever.

Opening prayer

God of steadfast love,
let the patient endurance of your martyrs
draw us to contemplate more deeply
the mystery of Christ,
and find there
the wellspring of courage and peace.
We make this prayer through Jesus Christ our Lord.

Acclamation

John 12:26

V/. Alleluia! Alleluia! Alleluia!
R/. Alleluia! Alleluia! Alleluia!
V/. 'Whoever serves me must follow me,
and where I am, there also shall my servant be,' says the Lord.
R/. Alleluia! Alleluia! Alleluia!

Intercession

Confirm, O God,
what you have wrought in us,
and preserve in the hearts of your people
the gifts of the Holy Spirit,
that they may not be ashamed
to confess the faith of Christ crucified,
but may fearlessly acknowledge him
who lives for ever and ever.

Prayer over the Gifts

Lord,
let us hallow your table with thanksgiving
as we proclaim the death of Jesus,
for in his sacrifice
all martyrdom finds its meaning and fulfilment.
We ask this through Christ our Lord.

Eucharistic Preface

It is truly right and just, our joy and our salvation,
always and everywhere to give you thanks,
Holy Father, eternal God,
through Jesus Christ your Son.

We remember in thanksgiving
those men and women
who stood forth as faithful to your name
and to the testimony of Jesus Christ,
and at the last did not hesitate
to confirm their faith by the shedding of their blood.

And so, with angels and all saints
we join the ageless hymn of your praise: Holy . . .

Prayer after Communion

God, our provider,
by the one bread and cup
you make us one with all those
who have stood firm in faith until the end.
Keep us strong in your love,
that we may walk in newness of life.
We ask this through Christ our Lord.

14 May Saint Matthias, Apostle

Matthias was chosen by prayer and the drawing of lots to occupy the place of Judas Iscariot (Acts 1:15–26) among the Apostles and witnesses to the resurrection.

Scripture-related opening prayer

God, you know every heart;
you chose Matthias to be enrolled
among the apostles and witnesses to the resurrection.

Let your blessing rest upon us,
and as you have chosen us
to walk in the way of Christ,

so let us be faithful to our calling
and at the last, receive your commendation.
We ask this through Jesus Christ,
who is one with you and the Holy Spirit,
now and for ever.

Opening prayer

God of our gladness,
let us rejoice in this feast
of your Apostle Saint Matthias.
We ask that as we honour him today,
so we may live as he lived,
and come to share with him in the resurrection
to which he bore such faithful witness.
We make this prayer through Jesus Christ our Lord.

Acclamation

John 15:16

V/. Alleluia! Alleluia! Alleluia!
R/. Alleluia! Alleluia! Alleluia!
V/. 'You did not choose me, I chose you,' says the Lord,
'and I appointed you to go out and bear fruit that will last.'
R/. Alleluia! Alleluia! Alleluia!

Intercession

Righteous God,
whose wisdom has called us to be your Church,
make and keep us faithful
as the stewards of your mysteries,
and bring us at the last
into the light of your glory.
We ask this through Christ our Lord.

Prayer over the Gifts

Accept from your people, Lord,
the sacrifice of praise and thanksgiving,
and confirm us in communion with all your saints.
We ask this through Christ our Lord.

Eucharistic Preface

We lift up our hearts to you,
God eternal, true and faithful;
to you we offer thanks and praise
through Jesus Christ your Son.

With wisdom and love you looked on Saint Matthias
and chose him to complete the number of the Apostles,
as one who had walked with your Son
and come to know the mystery of Christ.
You added his voice to the witness of the Twelve,
announcing to the world that Christ was risen,
and the heavenly kingdom prepared
for all men and women to enter.

And so, with angels and all saints,
we glorify your holy name: Holy . . .

Prayer after Communion

Generous God,
by these gifts, nourish your people
and strengthen them as witnesses to Christ,
so that they may inherit
the joy of the saints in light.
We ask this through Christ our Lord.

31 May The Visit of the Blessed Virgin Mary to Elizabeth

This feast was introduced into the Franciscan Calendar by Saint Bonaventure in the thirteenth century. In a typical Franciscan fashion, it celebrates the human emotions of Mary's visit to Elizabeth, and also the coming of the Holy Spirit of prophecy to reveal the presence of Christ and the grace given to the Virgin Mary.

Scripture-related opening prayer

God of wonders,
in the visitation of the blessed Virgin Mary
you brought joy to her kinswoman Elizabeth
as she greeted the mother of her Lord.

Let your Holy Spirit inspire in us
the same gladness as filled their meeting,
so that we may proclaim your greatness
as the God who exalts the lowly
and sets the needy in the place of princes.

This we ask through Jesus Christ,
who is one with you and the Holy Spirit
for ever and ever.

Opening prayer

Almighty and eternal God,
you inspired the Blessed Virgin Mary,
while carrying your Son in her womb,
to visit her cousin Elizabeth.
Grant that we may always follow
the prompting of the Holy Spirit
and be one with Mary
in proclaiming your greatness.
We ask this through Jesus Christ our Lord.

Acclamation

Luke 1:49

V/. The Mighty One has done great things for me;
and holy is his name.

Intercession

Be present in our midst, O God,
as you have promised to be with those who believe;
let your Church's prayer be heard
and your people's hands grow strong
to answer the needs of those
for whom we have offered our intercession.
We ask this through Christ our Lord.

Prayer over the Gifts

God of community,
as you brought Elizabeth and Mary together
in the praises of your mighty works,
so unite us now as we make thanksgiving
and give us the words to sing your praise.
We ask this through Christ our Lord.

Eucharistic Preface

It is truly right and just, our duty and our salvation,
always and everywhere to give you thanks,
Lord, holy Father, almighty and eternal God,
through Jesus Christ our Lord.

Through the prophetic words of Elizabeth
inspired by the Holy Spirit,
you revealed to us the greatness
bestowed on the Blessed Virgin Mary.
Rightly is she greeted as the blessed one,

because she had believed the promise of salvation;
rightly is she welcomed for her kindly visit,
and acclaimed as the mother of the Lord
by her who is to be the mother of his herald.

Therefore, with angels and saints,
we glorify your holy name: Holy . . .

Prayer after Communion

Let the Church proclaim your greatness, O God,
for you have done great things for the lowly.
John the Baptist leapt for joy
when he sensed the hidden presence of your Son.
Let your Church likewise rejoice
to recognize Christ in this sacrament.
We ask this through Christ our Lord.

PART SEVEN

TEXTS FOR EVENING PRAYER OF SATURDAY OR A SUNDAY VIGIL SERVICE

It is traditional in many Christian communities to begin the celebration of Sunday with Evening Prayer on Saturday night. Evening Prayer itself may take the form of a Vigil service for Sunday.

Saturday Evening Prayer may begin with a Service of Light. A Rite of Incense may also be used. Some texts to accompany these rites are given here. The texts for the Rite of Incense are based on hymns for Vespers in the service books of the Orthodox Church and the biblical texts of the Lent Lectionary. They are sung as verses with the refrain based on Psalm 141:2, as given in the first volume of this collection.

When the rites of Light and Incense are to be used with Evening Prayer or the Sunday Vigil, they should take place at the beginning of the service.

The Service of Light

(Common Worship – Daily Prayer (Church House Publishing 2002) also makes provision for this on pp. 84ff.)

The minister holds a lighted candle and opens the service with these words:

In the name of our Lord Jesus Christ,
light and peace be with you all.
All: And also with you.

Saturday or a Sunday Vigil Service

Lights are kindled as required.

For a suitable hymn, one of the following might be chosen:

Hail, gladdening light *(Hymns For Today's Church 275)*
O gladsome light *(New English Hymnal 247)*
O gracious light, Lord Jesus Christ *(Laudate 14)*
Light of gladness *(Laudate 15)*

or:

O Trinity of blessed light *(New English Hymnal 54)*
Christ, mighty Saviour *(Worship 681)*
Thy strong word didst cleave the darkness *(Worship 511)*
'I am the light of the world,' says the Lord *(Gather 510)*
The Light of Christ *(Gather 511)*

After the hymn, the following blessing of the light may be used:

Minister
Praise and blessing to our God,
at whose word the light shines,
the dawn breaks, the evening comes;
who gives the sun to rule the day,
the moon to mark the hours of night;
who set the constellations in their place
to adorn the vault of heaven
and show the passage of the seasons.
R/. Blessed be God for ever, Amen.

or:

Minister:
Christ, our Light:
R/. To you be glory for ever.
Christ, light of the world:
R/. To you be glory for ever.
Christ, light that shines in darkness:
R/. To you be glory for ever.

Blessing and honour and glory and power:
R/. To our God for ever and ever, Amen.

The Rite of Incense

Three sets of texts are given, the first for the Sundays of Lent, the second for other Sundays including those of Eastertime, and a third set for Pentecost Eve.

Lent

The First Sunday of Lent

Refrain:

Let my prayer— rise like in - - cense;
my up - lift - ed hands as the eve - ning sac - ri - fice.

Tone:

God fashioned Adam from the clay of earth
And in his nostrils breathed the breath of life;
In paradise God placed him, but he fell,
Lamenting now the glory he had lost: R/.

'I disobeyed God's word; tempted I fell.
An exile now, expelled from paradise,
With leaves for clothes, with garments made of skin
I sweat and toil to win my daily bread.   R/.

O paradise, O beauty unsurpassed!
Garden of God where saints and angels walk!

Remember me and pray for me to God,
That he restore me to the place of life.' R/.

Before the gate of Eden Adam wept,
So Adam's children fast and weep with him;
For Christ will welcome all who thus repent
And set their feet upon his living way. R/.

To grieving Adam Christ the Saviour speaks:
'That which my hand has made shall not be lost;
All that the Father gives me, comes to me,
And those who come, I will not turn away.' R/.

The Second Sunday of Lent

Refrain:

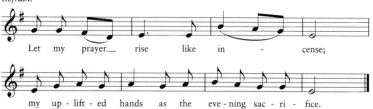

Let my prayer___ rise like in - cense; my up - lift - ed hands as the eve - ning sac - ri - fice.

Tone:

The grace of Christ our God has been revealed,
Whose gospel sheds its light upon us all,
Whose dying saves us from the curse of death,
Whose rising brings us to eternal life.

Year A
As Moses lifted up the serpent in the desert,
So must the Son of Man be lifted up;
That all who believe in him may not be lost
But have new birth into eternal life.

Year B
The glory that is yours as God's own Son
Shines from your holy and life-giving cross
On which you overthrew the power of death
And brought us resurrection and new life.

Year C
Our homeland is in heaven, and from heaven
The Lord will come, our Saviour Jesus Christ,
And he will change this lowly mortal body
Into the likeness of his glorious body.

You are the image of the unseen God,
The flawless mirror of God's glory bright,
Creator Word by whom all things were made,
In whom all things are reconciled to God.

Guide us, O Christ our God, throughout this Lent
That we may journey safely to the feast,
And reach the Passover of life and light
Which in your likeness fashions us anew.

The Third Sunday of Lent

Refrain:

Let my prayer rise like in - - cense;
my up - lift - ed hands as the eve - ning sac - ri - fice.

Tone:

The grace of Christ our God has been revealed,
Whose gospel sheds its light upon us all,
Whose dying saves us from the curse of death,
Whose rising brings us to eternal life.

Year A
The Fount of living water asks a drink
From her whom he created to receive
The gift of faith in God, the living One,
Who kindles in her heart the fire of love.

Year B
Your holy cross, O Christ our God, reveals
The Father's power and wisdom unsurpassed;
Your rising from the dead is our new life,
Your risen body is the living Temple.

Year C
Be merciful to us, Lord Jesus Christ,
As with the barren fig tree you were patient;
Grant us this Lenten time to change our heart
And turn again to you, the source of life.

You are the image of the unseen God,
The flawless mirror of God's glory bright,
Creator Word by whom all things were made,
In whom all things are reconciled to God.

Guide us, O Christ our God, throughout this Lent
That we may journey safely to the feast,
And reach the Passover of life and light
Which in your likeness fashions us anew.

The Fourth Sunday of Lent

Refrain:

Let my prayer rise like in - - cense;
my up - lift - ed hands as the eve - ning sac - ri - fice.

Tone:

The grace of Christ our God has been revealed,
Whose gospel sheds its light upon us all,
Whose dying saves us from the curse of death,
Whose rising brings us to eternal life.

Year A
The blind man washed and gained his sight and praised
The One whose healing word has spoken thus:
'For this he had been sightless, that in him
The works of God might be made manifest.'

Year B
As Moses lifted up the serpent in the desert,
So must the Son of Man be lifted up;
That all who believe in him may not be lost
But have new birth into eternal life.

Year C
The Father ran to kiss his son, while yet far off,
Restored him to his home and said 'Rejoice!
For this my son was dead and is alive,
My child was lost and now is found again.'

O Light undying, hear our evening praise,
For you have filled the universe with light;
Your light divine transforms our human flesh
And shines for ever, mirrored in your saints.

Guide us, O Christ our God, throughout this Lent
That we may journey safely to the feast,
And reach the Passover of life and light
Which in your likeness fashions us anew.

The Fifth Sunday of Lent

Refrain:

Let my prayer rise like in - - cense;
my up - lift - ed hands as the eve - ning sac - ri - fice.

Tone:

Shine out, O cross of Christ, life-giving tree
Where sorrow, tears and grief were wiped away;
Your wood has saved us from the sting of death,
And brought us to the glory of new life.

Year A
You wept, O Christ, for Lazarus your friend,
You raised him from his four days in the tomb;
You are the resurrection and the life,
Glory to you, life-giving Son of God!

Year B
Now has the Son of Man been glorified,
Now is God's judgement passed upon the world;
The seed that dies bursts into life anew,
For you, O Christ our God, have conquered death.

Year C
Your judgement, Christ our God, is full of mercy,
The adulterous woman you did not condemn;
As Lawgiver you cancelled her dread sentence
And set her free and bade her sin no more.

O Light undying, hear our evening praise,
For you have filled the universe with light;
Your light divine transforms our human flesh
And shines for ever, mirrored in your saints.

Guide us, O Christ our God, throughout this Lent
That we may journey safely to the feast,
And reach the Passover of life and light
Which in your likeness fashions us anew.

Palm Sunday

Refrain:
Let my prayer rise like in - - cense; my up-lift-ed hands as the eve-ning sac - ri - fice.

Tone:

Today the Holy Spirit gathers us together,
We lift your holy cross, O Saviour, saying:
'Blessed is he who comes in the name of the Lord!
Hosanna in the highest! Glory to our God!'

Today the eternal Word, Son of the Father,
Comes to Jerusalem seated on a donkey;
The Hebrew children waving palms and branches
Cry out and glorify the resurrection.

Let us, the Church of gentiles, also come
With Daughter Zion to sing and shout God's praise;
Behold the King! Behold the coming Saviour!
Blessed is he who comes in the name of God!

The songs of children welcome you, O Christ,
As they see you enter the holy City in triumph;
This is the promise of your coming reign
For us who praise your glorious resurrection.

Entering the holy City, O Christ our God,
You come to embrace your freely chosen passion;
And so, foretelling your rising from the dead
We cry aloud: 'Blessed are you, the living One!'

Blessed are you, our Saviour and our God,
Whose resurrection makes the angels sing;
Brings joy to Adam and all righteous souls
And opens wide the road to paradise.

Other Sundays including those of Eastertide

The Second Sunday of Easter

Refrain:

Let my prayer— rise like in - cense; my up - lift - ed hands as the eve - ning sac - ri - fice.

Tone:

O risen Lord, let this our evening prayer
Arise like fragrant incense in your sight;
You are the living One who died and rose
Revealing resurrection to the world.

Let all arise and circle Zion with joy
And glorify the One who rose from death;
The Christ, the living, true, eternal God
Who saved us from our sins by his own blood.

Let all adore the Lord and sing his praise,
And glorify the resurrection from the dead;
Christ is our Lord and God who trampled down
Our ancient and deceitful enemy.

Rejoice, O heaven! Let your trumpets sound!
Let earth's foundations shake with happy mirth!
For Christ by dying has destroyed our death,
Restoring life to Adam and his race.

To Christ who in the flesh bore death for us,
Who suffered and was buried and rose up;
We pray: 'Confirm your Church in truth and praise,
Give peace to all, O friend of humankind!'

The Third Sunday of Easter

Refrain:

Tone:

Come, let us worship Christ the Son of God,
The First-Begotten, now of Mary born,
Who by his own free will accepted death
And rose again to save and raise the lost.

By dying, Christ has trampled over death,
Death's might is now undone, its sting is crushed;
Let us adore the risen glorious Lord,
His third-day rising praise, his glory sing.

With all creation's powers let us praise
The rising of the Lord who saves our souls;
For he will come again to judge the world
Which his creating hand has formed and made.

The women came with myrrh, the Angel spoke:
'Why seek the Living here among the dead?
For just as he foretold, the Lord is risen,
The source of life is risen from the tomb.'

You burst the gates of death, broke down its doors,
Then from the darkness brought your people home;
Led by your hand they came forth into light,
Singing your praise, the Lord of endless life.

The Fourth Sunday of Easter

Refrain: Let my prayer rise like incense; my up-lift-ed hands as the eve-ning sac-ri-fice.

Tone:

You broke the grip of death, O Christ our Saviour,
When on the cross you foiled our ancient foe;
By faith you save us and to faith you call us,
Praise be to you, Redeemer of the world!

Your rising floods the universe with glory;
The way to Paradise is opened wide;
With sounds of joy the whole creation echoes,
Praise be to you, Redeemer of the world!

Down to the place of death the living Saviour
Descended to announce the gracious words:
'Take heart, for I have conquered, I am risen!
I am the resurrection and the life.'

Amid your Church, O Christ our God, we bless you
And offer you our evening hymns of praise:
O Christ the friend of humankind, the risen One,
O save us, grant us peace and raise us up!

We praise the Father, Son and Holy Spirit,
The uncreated Godhead do we praise;
True God, in essence One and Undivided,
Who reigns for ever, Trinity sublime!

The Fifth Sunday of Easter

Refrain:

Let my prayer rise like in - - cense;
my up - lift - ed hands as the eve - ning sac - ri - fice.

Tone:

Your life-bestowing cross we praise and honour,
We glorify your rising, Christ our God;
Through them you have renewed our fallen nature
And brought us back to walk your holy ways.

Upon the cross-tree you, the Judge, were seated,
The former tree's dark sentence to annul;
Descending to death's prison, you, most mighty,
Shattered its doors and set its prisoners free.

By dying you destroyed our death, O Saviour;
You broke the bonds of death, O Christ our God;
You freed us from corruption by your mercy
And life immortal you have brought to all.

Come, let us sing our Saviour's resurrection,
And with the Angels praise and thank the Lord;
Who brought us out of death to incorruption,
And shed his glorious light on humankind.

Your coming from the Father is eternal,
Your Incarnation is beyond all power to tell;
Your advent with the dead strikes death with terror,
For now you have destroyed its pain and fear.

The Sixth Sunday of Easter

Refrain:

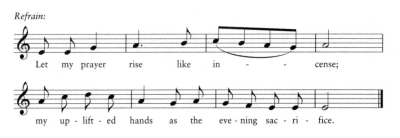

Let my prayer rise like in - - cense;
my up - lift - ed hands as the eve - ning sac - ri - fice.

Tone:

You broke the power of death, Lord Jesus Christ,
When on the cross you offered up your life;
And by your glorious rising from the dead,
You led us forth from darkness into light.

Led to the slaughter like a spotless lamb
You are our Passover of life and peace;
You went into the darkest realm of death
to set its captives free and lead them forth.

Christ who has made all things, seen and unseen,
In love for all has suffered in the flesh;
And in the flesh is risen from the dead,
The promise of a glory yet to be.

O Light undying, hear our evening praise,
For you have filled the universe with light;
Your light divine transforms our human flesh
And shines for ever, mirrored in your saints.

Glory to you, our Saviour and our Lord,
Whose resurrection makes the Angels sing,
Brings joy to Adam and all righteous souls
And opens wide the way to paradise.

The Seventh Sunday of Easter

Refrain:

Let my prayer rise like in - - cense;
my up - lift - ed hands as the eve - ning sac - ri - fice.

Tone:

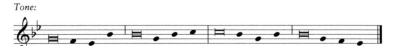

When you were lifted high upon the cross,
You raised up those who sat enchained in death,
For you alone are free of death's dominion;
O risen Saviour, source of light, have mercy.

Today the risen Lord fills earth with gladness,
Who trampled death and rose as he had said;
O Christ who dwell in light, the fount of life,
O risen Saviour, source of light, have mercy.

Where can we flee to hide ourselves from you?
Not up to heaven for there you make your dwelling;
Nor to the grave, for there you conquered death.
O risen Saviour, source of light, have mercy.

We sing our hymn of praise to you, O Christ,
Who by your death destroyed the power of death
And, rising, promised glory to all flesh;
O risen Saviour, source of light, have mercy.

Lord Jesus, first-begotten from the dead,
The first-fruits of God's harvesting to come,
You will return in glory as the judge;
O risen Saviour, source of light, have mercy.

The Eve of Pentecost

Let my prayer rise like in - - cense;

my up - lift - ed hands as the eve - ning sac - ri - fice.

O come and let us sing for joy to God!
O heavenly powers, praise the risen Lord
Who gave the Holy Spirit from on high:
O Maker, Saviour, glory be to you!

You filled your Church, O Christ, with gifts of speech,
Speech to proclaim the wonders of your love,
Words that would reach the farthest ends of earth,
Words to announce your presence and your peace.

The Holy Spirit comes to do your work,
To loosen tongues in prophecy and praise,
To set apart a priesthood, teach true wisdom,
And bind your Church together into one.

Today we see the true and holy light,
The Holy Spirit we have all received;
We find true faith in worship of one God,
The Father, Son, and Spirit, evermore.

Glory to you, O Christ, eternal Son,
By whom the Holy Spirit is outpoured;
Receive our evening prayer of joyful praise
And save us all, O friend of humankind.

Prayer to conclude the Rite of Incense

Lent Sundays
God of all faithfulness,
you showed your power
on the night you rescued your people from slavery.
Show that same power now to us;
deliver us from sin,
then, on that holy night
which we await with all your children,
we will sing your glory in full freedom,
through Jesus Christ our Lord.

Easter Sundays
Lord our God,
your Son, risen from the dead,
is the Bridegroom who comes by night
and invites us to his wedding feast.
Keep alive in us the flame of faith,
that we may hasten towards the kingdom
which you have promised will be ours,
for ever and ever.

Pentecost Eve
God of light,
on this evening of praise we thank you
for having poured out the Spirit of Truth
upon your Church.
May the Spirit disperse the darkness in our hearts
that we may more and more live
as true children of the light,
through Jesus, the Christ, our Lord.

If Evening Prayer is to form the rest of the service, it begins with the Word of God – the Psalmody as set out on p. 41 of Common Worship. *The Readings will be those appointed in the Daily Office Lectionary.*

The Ministry of the Word

If a Service of the Word is to be celebrated, it follows the Service of Light (and that of Incense) with the Collect and the rest as outlined on p. 24 of Common Worship.

If the Saturday Evening Vigil is a regular part of worship, then readings may be chosen on a 'continuous reading' basis from one of the available lectionaries.

Otherwise, one option for the choice of readings might be to choose from the readings suggested in the Lectionary for the years other than that which is currently under way. The Second and Third Service options might also be used, if appropriate.

Between the readings, canticles may be used (see the selection in Common Worship – Daily Prayer *(Church House Publishing 2002, pp. 493–575), followed by times of silence. If appropriate, the Scripture-related opening prayer for the Sunday might be used after the responsorial canticle.*

A psalm or psalms may be recited before the readings, or between them as an alternative to canticles. If psalm prayers are desired, the psalms should be followed by a time of silence and the psalm prayer. Common Worship – Daily Prayer *has psalm prayers attached to the psalms in the Psalter, pp. 575ff. It is appropriate for people to sit for the psalms and prayers.*

The Taizé responses might be useful aids to prayer during the readings at the Vigil.

If non-Scripture readings are desired to follow the Scripture readings, these might be taken from Celebrating the Seasons *(Canterbury Press 1999) or another collection of spiritual readings, such as:* From the Fathers to the Churches *(Collins 1983) or* Christ our Light – Patristic Readings on Gospel Themes *(Exordium Books 1981), which follows the Roman Gospel lectionary for Sundays and so, in great part, the* Common Worship *Sunday Lectionary.*

The readings should conclude with the Gospel of the coming Sunday, preceded by the acclamation Alleluia *with appropriate verse, or a suitable hymn.*

The outline of A Service of the Word *allows for a homily, but this is not necessary if a reading from the Patristic tradition appropriate to the Gospel has been chosen.*

Long readings may be read in short portions with silence between them rather than as one single extract.

The Conclusion of the Vigil

The Vigil may end with the hymn Te Deum Laudamus, *followed by the Collect of the Sunday, a blessing and dismissal.*

PART EIGHT

THE VIGILS OF ASCENSION DAY AND PENTECOST

If a special First Evening Prayer for Ascension is required, it may begin with a Service of Light, or a Rite of Incense, or both.

The Service of Light

The Easter Candle is lit before the service. The president and ministers enter. The president begins the service.

President
The light and peace of Jesus Christ be with you all.
R/. And also with you.

A hymn of light may be sung:

Hail, gladdening light *(Hymns For Today's Church 275)*
O gladsome light *(New English Hymnal 247)*
O gracious light, Lord Jesus Christ *(Laudate 14)*
Light of gladness *(Laudate 15)*

Prayer

God of glory,
in the risen and ascended Christ
you have led us out of darkness
into your own wonderful light.
Awaken our sleeping hearts,

give light to those who have lost their way
and make the resplendent light of Christ
shine on us all.
We ask this in his name, our Saviour,
now and for ever.
R/. Amen.

The Rite of Incense

Refrain:

Let my prayer— rise like in - cense; my up - lift - ed hands as the eve - ning sac - ri - fice.

Tone:

The Holy Spirit commands the heavenly powers:
'Lift up your heads, you everlasting doors!'
And one who was made lower than the angels
Is raised above them to the Father's glory.

The Lord is taken up into the heavens
That he might send the Advocate into the world;
The heavens prepare his throne, the clouds his mount,
On which he will return to judge the earth.

We glorify you, eternal Son of God,
We praise your resurrection from the dead,
We honour your ascension into heaven;
Compassionate One, have pity on your people.

243

The apostles saw you, raised above the clouds,
They wept with lamentation and with grief:
'Leave us not orphans, but send the Holy Spirit
To fill us with the living light of God.'

You have exalted our mortal nature, O Christ,
And seated our humanity on God's throne.
Angels are seized with wonder, heaven trembles
To glorify your mercy on us all.

Prayer to conclude the Service of Incense

We give thanks to you, God and Father,
through Jesus your beloved Son.
Ascending to your right hand,
he draws all people to himself.
Let us share his joy,
so that your Church may grow
in all ways into him, our head,
who makes us one,
now and for ever.
R/. Amen.

A Vigil for Pentecost

The Vigil of Pentecost may be celebrated with as much festivity as the Easter Vigil, including a celebration of the Eucharist.

Or, more simply, it might take the form of an extended Evening Prayer. In this case the services of Light and Incense may form the beginning of the service.

The lessons may be selected from the suggestions given below.

Or, it might be celebrated as suggested, only without the Eucharist. In this case it would conclude with prayers of intercession after the Gospel, followed by the canticle *Te Deum Laudamus* and the Collect.

Like the Easter Vigil, the Vigil of Pentecost is an appropriate occasion for the baptism and confirmation of adults. If this is done, the Ministry of the Word should be followed by the Service of Baptism, as at the Easter Vigil, and should conclude with the Service of Baptism followed by the Eucharist.

The Vigil begins with the Service of Light.

The Easter candle is lit before the service. The president and ministers enter. The president begins the service.

President
The light and peace of Jesus Christ be with you all.
R/. And also with you.

A hymn of light may be sung:

Hail, gladdening light (Hymns For Today's Church *275)*
O gladsome light (New English Hymnal *247)*
O gracious light, Lord Jesus Christ (Laudate *14)*
Light of gladness (Laudate *15)*

Or a Pentecost hymn of light, such as:

Rejoice, the year upon its way (New English Hymnal *136)*
Come down, O Love divine (New English Hymnal *137)*
Come, thou Holy Spirit, come (New English Hymnal *139)*

Candles are lit as appropriate during the hymn. This Collect may conclude the Service of Light:

God, faithful and true,
your Son, risen from the dead,
has fulfilled your promises of old
and sent the Holy Spirit upon his disciples.

Let the fire of the Spirit
keep the flame of faith burning in our hearts,
that by its light we may hasten
with joyful steps towards the wedding feast
where you will be all in all,
for ever and ever.

*If the Rite of Incense is to be celebrated, see the texts given in
Part Seven, pp. 238–9.*

The Ministry of the Word

The president says:

Dear friends in Christ,
the book of the Acts of the Apostles teaches us
that after the Ascension of Jesus,
the apostles met in constant prayer
with Mary the mother of Jesus and his brothers.
They were awaiting that power from on high,
promised by the Lord,
by which they would be witnesses to the gospel
everywhere on earth.

Let us listen tonight
to the wonderful works of God.
For God has sent the Spirit of adoption
by which we cry out 'Abba! Father!'
and God is preparing us to be his witnesses
that Jesus is Lord, to the glory of God the Father.

*The following Old Testament readings are suggested, either all
of them or a choice:*

*First Reading: Genesis 11:1–9
At Babel, God confounds the languages of the earth.*

Responsorial Psalm 47

Collect
Almighty God,
you have given us this holy season of fifty days
to celebrate the new life which is ours
in the Passover of Christ.
Through the power of your Spirit,
gather the diversity of nations and tongues
and make them one body
to praise your glorious name.
We ask this through Jesus Christ our Lord.

Second Reading: Exodus 19:1–7, 16–25
At Sinai, God prepares to pronounce the Law.

Responsorial Psalm 50:1–6

Collect

Write upon our hearts, O God,
what once you wrote on tablets of stone
for your holy people;
so that by your Holy Spirit
we may know your law
inscribed within us,
and in our thoughts and actions
we may keep and reverence the same.
We ask this through Jesus Christ our Lord.

Third Reading: Ezekiel 37:1–14
The dry bones hear the word of the Lord.

Responsorial Psalm 98:1–6

Collect

Over the chaos of our abandonment,
the dryness of exhausted hope,

breathe, O God,
the Spirit that makes us living beings,
the mighty wind of your creation.
Stand us on our feet
and name us as your own;
revive what is withered in us
and give strength to what is weak,
so that your people, as one great multitude,
may witness to your steadfastness and truth.
We ask this through Jesus Christ our Lord.

Fourth Reading: Joel 3:1–15
God promises to pour out the Spirit on all flesh.

Responsorial psalm 104:1–4, 24, 27–30

Collect

God of wonders,
you transformed the apostles
by your Spirit of freedom.
From being afraid,
they announced your kingdom
and throwing open their locked doors
they took up their mission with joy.
Visit your Church at prayer this day
and let the Holy Spirit breathe confidence and faith
into those who believe in Jesus,
our Lord, now and for ever.

New Testament Reading: Romans 8:22–27
The Spirit expresses our prayers in indescribable ways.

Responsorial Psalm 117

Before the Gospel, a suitable hymn may be sung.

Acclamation

V/. Come, Spirit of God,
fill the hearts of your people
and enkindle in them the fire of your love.

Gospel Reading: John 7:37–39
Fountains of living water

*The Service of Baptism and Confirmation may follow the
sermon.*

Intercession

Gather your Church, O God,
through the coming of the Holy Spirit,
so that your people may be wholly dedicated
to the service of your praise.
We ask this through Christ our Lord.

If the Eucharist is celebrated, these prayers might be used:

Prayer over the Gifts

Bless your table, Lord,
by the coming of the Holy Spirit,
and teach us, through love of one another,
to be true witnesses of your peace.
We ask this through Christ our Lord.

Eucharistic Preface

It is truly right and just, our duty and our salvation,
to give you thanks and praise, O God,
as we celebrate the day of Pentecost.

In the first days of your Church
the Holy Spirit imparted to all peoples

the knowledge of your Godhead
and speech to announce your wonders.
Through many gifts that differ
the Spirit works a wonderful unity:
in the variety of what is bestowed
the Spirit imparts all things in wisdom:
indeed it is the selfsame Spirit
who creates many tongues to proclaim your word
and bestows the faith which binds them into one.

And so, in the joy of this Passover,
earth and heaven resound with gladness;
the angels and the powers of all creation
sing the ageless hymn of your glory: Holy . . .

Prayer after Communion

God most high,
who bestow the gifts of heaven
upon your exultant Church,
make the presence of your Spirit
flourish in vigour among us,
that this spiritual food and drink
may bring us to eternal redemption.
We ask this through Jesus Christ our Lord.

PART NINE

ASH WEDNESDAY

Ash Wednesday, the first day of Lent, takes its name from the ceremony of ashes which is traditionally performed at the Eucharist, but which might also be done at another service. The ceremony of ashes dates from the early Middle Ages, when people did public penance in church. Penance, like prayer, was a communal event, so such people became known as 'the Order of Penitents'.

These Penitents were excluded from the Eucharist during Lent. To show this they were marked with ashes as Lent began. On Maundy Thursday they gathered with the Bishop for a Liturgy of Reconciliation. Penitential devotion was popular and eventually everyone wore ashes on what became the first day of Lent. The prayers for Ash Wednesday assume that this day is kept as a day of fasting.

It is traditional to make ashes from palms blessed on Palm Sunday of the previous year.

Two forms are proposed here for an Ash Wednesday service. The first form is intended to be used at the Eucharist, the second is a simple form of Evening Prayer.

The Ash Wednesday Eucharist

The president greets the people as usual. This introduction may be used:

President
Dear friends in Christ,
the gospel of Christ calls us to turn our back on sin

251

and reject everything that keeps us apart from God.
As we begin the season of Lent,
let us remember our mortal frailty,
acknowledge our sinfulness and turn to the Lord,
for with God is the fullness of redemption.

Let us pray.

God of compassion,
you welcome all who turn to you
and grant forgiveness to all who repent.
Pour out your blessing
on those who are marked with these ashes,
so that they may faithfully observe
the season of Lent,
and come with a heart made clean
to celebrate the Passover of Christ your Son,
who is alive, now and for ever.

or:

Holy and merciful God,
you desire not the death of a sinner,
but rather the sinner's repentance and life.
Bless these ashes,
which we, who are dust,
will place on our heads.
Let this outward mark
be imprinted on our hearts,
so that we may be faithful to the observance of Lent,
receive pardon for our sins
and be renewed in the likeness of the risen Christ.
We ask this in the name of Jesus the Lord.

*Blessed water may be sprinkled on the ashes. Ashes are placed on
everyone's head. These words may accompany the marking with
ashes:*

Turn away from sin
and be faithful to the Gospel.

or:

Remember, man/woman, that you are dust
and to dust you will return.

*Suitable psalms or chants may accompany the giving of the
ashes. Afterwards, the ministers wash their hands. The Eucharist
continues with the Opening Prayer.*

Scripture-related opening prayer

Gracious God,
you give us this time of salvation
to turn from sin and seek your face.
We ask you to cleanse and purify our hearts;
rouse us to prayer, self-denial
and service of our neighbour,
that we may know the joy of your kingdom
and have our treasure in heaven.
We ask this through Jesus Christ,
who is one with you and the Holy Spirit,
now and for ever.

Opening prayer

Grant us, Lord, the grace
to begin this campaign of Christian service with a holy fast,
so that as we prepare to fight against the spirit of evil,
we may be armed with the strength of self-discipline.
We make this prayer through Jesus Christ our Lord.

or:

O God,
you have made us for yourself,
and against your longing there is no defence.

Mark us with your love,
and release in us a passion for your justice
in our disfigured world;
that we may turn from our guilt and face you,
our heart's desire.
Through Jesus Christ.

Acclamation

'Alleluia' is not used during Lent. In its place an acclamation is said or sung.

Years ABC: Psalm 51:10
V/. Christ our Saviour, glory to you!
R/. Christ our Saviour, glory to you!
V/. Create in me a clean heart, O God,
and put a new and right spirit within me.
R/. Christ our Saviour, glory to you!

Intercession

Most loving God,
pour out the spirit of repentance
on those who bend the knee before your glory,
and in your compassion, grant to them
the forgiveness promised to those who turn to you.
We ask this through Christ our Lord.

Prayer over the Gifts

As Lent begins, O God,
we prepare your table.
Let fasting nourish our spirit,
let prayer fill us with blessing
and let works of love
fortify us as your holy people.
We ask this through Christ our Lord.

Ash Wednesday

Eucharistic Preface

It is truly right and just, our joy and our salvation,
always and everywhere to give you thanks,
God most holy, living and true.

You refresh us with bodily food
but also with food for the spirit;
you desire us to live not by bread alone
but by the nourishment of your every word.
In this way, both by eating and by fasting
are we sustained and fed.
As you strengthen the body with food and drink,
so through abstinence and the works of love
you strengthen and renew the soul.
You have consecrated this Lent for us,
to bring us health of mind and body,
and turn us again to you
through Jesus Christ our Lord.

Through him, therefore,
with all the powers of heaven,
we glorify your holy name: Holy . . .

Prayer after Communion

Merciful God,
be our strength and sustenance
in the sacrament we share,
so that as we fast, we may be filled
with the gentleness of your healing love.
We ask this through Jesus Christ our Lord.

An Ash Wednesday Evening Prayer

For the burning of incense in this service a large bowl is required,
filled with dry sand, with a small metal bowl set in the sand for
the charcoal. The bowl should stand in a place where everyone
can access it.

Ashes should be ready in a suitable place.

The minister may greet the people:

V/. Grace, mercy and peace be with you, from Jesus Christ.
R/. And also with you.

Minister:
Dear friends,
the gospel of Christ calls us to turn our back on sin;
and reject everything that separates us from God.
As we begin the season of Lent,
let us keep in mind our mortal frailty,
acknowledge our sinfulness and turn to the Lord,
in whom is perfect goodness and from whom comes true
forgiveness.

A suitable chant is sung, such as:

or the Taizé response 'O Lord hear my prayer'.

Ash Wednesday

With these verses from Psalm 141:

Refrain:

Tone:

Lord, I call to you, make haste to hear me;
listen to my voice as I cry out before you. R/.

Lord, set a watch before my mouth;
a guard at the door of my lips. R/.

Do not let my heart turn to evil;
to works of wickedness with the wicked. R/.

To you, O Lord God, I turn my eyes;
in you I trust, do not reject me. R/.

Keep me from the trap they set for me;
and let me escape them always. R/.

or else this version:

Refrain:

Hear us O Lord, have mer-cy up-on us, for we have sinned a-gainst you.

Tone:

Lord, I call to you, make haste to hear me;
listen to my voice as I cry out before you.   R/.

Let my prayer rise before you like incense;
my uplifted hands as the evening sacrifice.   R/.

Lord, set a watch before my mouth;
a guard at the door of my lips.   R/.

Do not let my heart turn to evil;
to works of wickedness with the wicked.   R/.

To you, O Lord God, I turn my eyes;
in you I trust, do not reject me.   R/.

Keep me from the trap they set for me;
and let me escape them always.   R/.

During the singing of this Psalm, the congregation come and place incense on the charcoal. Then the minister says this Collect:

God most high,
let our prayer of repentance
rise before you with the smoke of incense,
and let your mercy descend upon us:
through Jesus Christ,
our Saviour, now and for ever.

The Office Hymn is sung:

(Another suitable melody is 'Tallis' Canon', New English Hymnal 244.)

Lord God and Maker of us all,
Accept and bless this Lent we keep;
And give the strength to persevere
Throughout the holy forty days.

You search and weigh the hearts of all,
You know how weak and frail we are;
O turn to us that we may turn
To seek your healing power again.

The sins are ours that we confess,
The pardon and the peace are yours;
Compassion is your name, and love,
O touch us with your gentle hand.

Give us the strength to keep the fast
With joy and peace and self-control;
To fast from sin as well as food,
True Lent for body and for soul.

Hear us, O holy Trinity,
To you the one true God we cry;
And through this fast prepare for us
A treasure safe with you on high. Amen.

Psalmody

The psalms appointed for Ash Wednesday evening may be recited or sung. If only one psalm is used, a good choice might be Psalm 39.

Suitable Old and New Testament lessons from an appropriate lectionary may be read. The Magnificat *and* Nunc Dimittis *are sung or recited as usual.*

Ash Wednesday

After the Nunc Dimittis, *the minister blesses the ashes as follows:*

My dear brothers and sisters in Christ,
let us ask God to bless us, our wearing of these ashes,
and our observance of these days of Lent.

Let us pray.

God of compassion,
you receive all who turn to you
and grant forgiveness to all who repent.
Pour out your blessing
on those who are marked by these ashes,
so that they may faithfully observe
the season of Lent,
and come with a heart made clean
to celebrate the Passover of Christ your Son,
who is alive, now and for ever.

or:

God, tender and merciful,
you desire not the death of a sinner,
but rather the sinner's repentance and life.
Bless these ashes,
which we who are dust
will place on our heads.
Let this outward mark
be imprinted on our hearts,
so that we may be faithful to the observance of Lent,
gain pardon for our sins
and be renewed in the likeness of the risen Christ.
We ask this in the name of Jesus Christ our Lord.

Blessed water may be sprinkled on the ashes. The ashes are imposed on everyone's head. These words may accompany the imposition:

Turn away from sin
and be faithful to the gospel.

or:

Remember, man/woman, that you are dust
and to dust you will return.

The Imposition of Ashes is followed by a silence for reflection.

Then the Evening Intercession is offered. The minister says:

God hears our pleading, God answers our prayer.
In repentance and faith let us turn to the Lord:

V/. Lord, have mercy;
R/. Christ, have mercy;
V/. Lord, have mercy.

Our Father . . .

V/. Lord, give strength to your people:
R/. Bless our Lent with your peace.
V/. All humankind must appear before you:
R/. Free them from guilt and sin.
V/. Save the downtrodden and oppressed:
R/. Let the poor and needy bless your name.
V/. You are the Father of the fatherless:
R/. Protect the lonely, orphans and bereaved.
V/. You are the fountain of living water:
R/. Bring life to all who have died in Christ.

The Collect for Ash Wednesday may be used here, with other collects of Evening Prayer, if desired.

PART TEN

THE WAY OF THE CROSS

*The prayer known as the 'Way' (or 'Stations') 'of the Cross'
became part of Roman Catholic devotion in the seventeenth and
eighteenth centuries. Its origins, however, are much older.*

*From the fourth century, pilgrims came to Jerusalem to pray at
the holy places associated with the death and resurrection of
Jesus. Among these was the traditional route taken by him as he
carried the cross from the headquarters of Pontius Pilate to
Golgotha.*

*Pilgrims would walk the route and tell the story, stopping at
intervals to read, sing and pray. These stops ('stations') were
in time associated with a series of events, some recounted in
the Passion narratives of the Gospels, others arising from the
imagination of the participants but nevertheless having echoes in
Scripture.*

*After the Muslim conquest of the Holy Land, pilgrimages
became more difficult as the Middle Ages went on. The Francis-
cans, traditional 'guardians' of the Holy Places, began to organ-
ize these pilgrim processions so that they could be held anywhere.
Often they took place out of doors and might occupy a whole
urban community for a day, like a sort of simple mystery play.
Eventually, the number of stations became fixed at fourteen. The
practice spread all over the Catholic Church in the seventeenth
and eighteenth centuries. Then, it became normal to hold the
service in church and the events associated with the stations were
depicted on the church walls, sometimes with a simple cross,
more often with a picture or statue of the event commemorated.*

*More recently, the Way of the Cross has proved itself to be an
opportunity for invention and creativity. Texts, readings, songs*

and prayers have been evolved for all sorts of groups and occasions. *Stations of the Cross for women, for people with HIV/AIDS, for the oppressed and 'disappeared' of Latin America, and many other forms have been created. Clearly this devotion to the Suffering of Christ speaks powerfully to a world where the suffering of so many is so prevalent.*

The Way of the Cross is bodily, repetitive prayer. Ideally, the congregation processes from station to station. At each station, the congregation gathers, kneels for prayer, then stands to listen to the Gospel or other biblical reading and prays before moving on. In this way a rhythm is established.

Two forms of the service are given here. The first is based on the traditional series of stations, with simple readings and prayers. The second is based on a set of stations which has been used by Pope John Paul II on Good Friday in Rome for several years. These are scriptural stations, omitting the traditional third, seventh and ninth (the falls), the fourth (Jesus meets his mother), and the sixth (Veronica).

The Way of the Cross: Traditional Form

This is a processional service, so the whole congregation should be encouraged to walk and gather at each station. A cross should be carried at the head of the procession, and lighted candles may accompany it.

Each station should be identified by a simple wooden cross set at eye level, perhaps with a light burning in front of it. In a large building it might be possible to erect each station as a freestanding cross, possibly with a depiction of the event attached as a banner. The space should be as uncluttered as possible, to allow movement and gathering around each station.

Ideally, two readers are required to read the Gospel readings alternately. Between the stations, verses of a hymn may be sung. The traditional hymn is *Stabat Mater* – 'At the cross her station keeping', *New English Hymnal* 97.

Other suitable hymns are 'My song is love unknown' *(New English Hymnal* 86) and 'Lift high the cross' *(Laudate* 389). Simple congregational settings of 'Lamb of God' from the Eucharist may also be used.

Before the Procession begins, the minister may introduce the service with the sign of the cross:

Minister: In the name of the Father, and of the Son, and of the Holy Spirit.
R/. Amen.

The minister and people recite alternately:

V/. Lord, have mercy:
R/. Lord, have mercy.
V/. Christ, have mercy:
R/. Christ, have mercy.
V/. Lord, have mercy:
R/. Lord, have mercy.

All then recite the Lord's Prayer.

The minister may say:

The way of the cross is a journey, made in the Holy Spirit.
That same Spirit burned in the heart of Christ as he bore his
passion and burns in the memory of the Church as we recall his
sufferings.

In this procession, we pray with our bodies,
our feet walking in the footsteps of our Saviour.
By walking, we enact our journey of faith
which began when we were baptized into Christ's death.
Let us pray that this commemoration of his sufferings
will train us to accept the challenge of his teaching,
and fill us with the hope of resurrection.

The Way of the Cross

Let us be still for a moment,
and name the cross that we are carrying.
Let us name also the many forms of the cross
carried by the poor, the oppressed and the sick,
in union with Christ.

Silent prayer

Collect

God of compassion, look upon your people,
for whose sake your Son Jesus Christ
freely chose to undergo the torment of the cross;
who now is alive, in one glory with you and the Holy Spirit,
now and for ever.
R/. Amen.

The procession moves to the first station, singing the verse(s) of a hymn. When the people have gathered, a reader says:

The first station on the way of the cross – where Jesus is condemned to death.

All kneel. The reader says: We adore you, O Christ, and we bless you:
All reply: Because by your holy cross you have redeemed the world.

The reader reads Luke 23:20–25.

A response to the reading should be used at each station. An appropriate chant is the Taizé response 'Jesus, remember me when you come into your kingdom.'

All pause in silence for a moment. Some brief intercessory prayers appropriate to the station may be offered at this point.

The minister concludes the station by reciting this Collect:

Christ, our Saviour,
judge of heaven and earth,
you allowed yourself to be put on trial
and condemned at human hands.
Give us courage to live by your justice,
so that we may face your judgement without fear;
for you are our redeemer,
now and for ever.
R/. Amen.

*The procession moves to the second station, singing the hymn
chosen. When all have gathered, a reader announces:*

The second station – where Jesus takes up the cross.

V/. We adore you, O Christ, and we bless you:
R/. Because by your holy cross you have redeemed the world.

The reader reads John 19:14, 17.

The response is sung, as above.

Silence is kept; intercession may be offered.

Collect

Christ, embrace us
with your steadfast love,
that we may take up the cross
as companions of all who bear heavy burdens,
and walk with them in your footsteps;
for you are the Saviour,
now and for ever.
R/. Amen.

The Way of the Cross

The procession moves to the third station, singing the hymn chosen. When all have gathered, a reader announces:

The third station – where Jesus falls for the first time.

V/. We adore you, O Christ, and we bless you:
R/. Because by your holy cross you have redeemed the world.

The reader reads Psalm 143:3, 4.

The response is sung, as above.

Silence is kept; intercession may be offered.

Collect

Jesus,
you freely chose
to be crushed beneath the world's violence.
Give us courage to stand
with those who have no choice but to suffer,
so that they may never suffer alone;
for you are our strength,
now and for ever.
R/. Amen.

The procession moves to the fourth station, singing the hymn chosen. When all have gathered, a reader announces:

The fourth station – where Jesus meets his sorrowful mother.

V/. We adore you, O Christ, and we bless you:
R/. Because by your holy cross you have redeemed the world.

The reader reads Luke 2:33–35.

The response is sung, as above.

Silence is kept; intercession may be offered.

Collect

Let your compassion, O Christ,
embrace the sorrows of this broken world,
that the night which passes in weeping
may be transformed by your passion
into the morning of joy and gladness,
for you are our Saviour,
now and for ever.
R/. Amen.

The procession moves to the fifth station, singing the hymn chosen. When all have gathered, a reader announces:

The fifth station – where Simon of Cyrene is forced to bear the cross.

V/. We adore you, O Christ, and we bless you:
R/. Because by your holy cross you have redeemed the world.

The reader reads Matthew 27:32.

The response is sung, as above.

Silence is kept; intercession may be offered.

Collect

Christ, our strength,
let us not grow weary
as we walk the way of the cross,
but sustain us and keep us faithful,
so that the burden may be light
and the yoke easy,
since it is carried on your shoulders,
for you are our Saviour,
now and for ever.
R/. Amen.

The Way of the Cross

The procession moves to the sixth station, singing the hymn chosen. When all have gathered, a reader announces:

The sixth station – where Veronica wipes the face of Jesus.

V/. We adore you, O Christ, and we bless you:
R/. Because by your holy cross you have redeemed the world.

The reader reads Matthew 25:37–40.

The response is sung, as above.

Silence is kept; intercession may be offered.

Collect

Jesus, whose face we desire to see,
teach us compassion
as you reveal yourself in the poor and needy;
bestir our hearts to serve them,
so that we may face you without fear,
our Saviour and Redeemer,
now and for ever.
R/. Amen.

The procession moves to the seventh station, singing the hymn chosen. When all have gathered, a reader announces:

The seventh station – where Jesus falls for the second time.

V/. We adore you, O Christ, and we bless you:
R/. Because by your holy cross you have redeemed the world.

The reader reads Isaiah 53:4–6.

The response is sung, as above.

Silence is kept; intercession may be offered.

Collect

Christ, eternal Word,
who took upon you
our human weakness even unto death;
be here for us, and for all who need your strength,
so that in falling, we may not abandon the way,
nor lose hope when close to despair.
This we ask for your sake,
our Saviour, now and for ever.
R/. Amen.

*The procession moves to the eighth station, singing the hymn
chosen. When all have gathered, a reader announces:*

The eighth station – where Jesus meets the women of Jerusalem.

V/. We adore you, O Christ, and we bless you:
R/. Because by your holy cross you have redeemed the world.

The reader reads Luke 23:27–31.

The response is sung, as above.

Silence is kept; intercession may be offered.

Collect

Jesus, our brother,
let this contemplation of your sufferings
make us compassionate to all who suffer,
so that in care and concern for them
we may give you worship that is genuine,
and practise a religion that is true and faultless;
for you are our Saviour
now and for ever.
R/. Amen.

The procession moves to the ninth station, singing the hymn chosen. When all have gathered, a reader announces:

The ninth station – where Jesus falls for the third time.

V/. We adore you, O Christ, and we bless you:
R/. Because by your holy cross you have redeemed the world.

The reader reads Psalm 143:3–4.

The response is sung, as above.

Silence is kept; intercession may be offered.

Collect

Christ, our lover,
you have plumbed the depths of darkness
and walked in the shadow
of sorrows that we dare not name.
Lift us up when we stumble and fall,
so that in time of failure
we may never let go of you,
our Saviour, now and for ever.
R/. Amen.

The procession moves to the tenth station, singing the hymn chosen. When all have gathered, a reader announces:

The tenth station – where Jesus is stripped of his garments.

V/. We adore you, O Christ, and we bless you:
R/. Because by your holy cross you have redeemed the world.

The reader reads John 19:23–24.

The response is sung, as above.

Silence is kept; intercession may be offered.

The Way of the Cross

Collect

Christ, deprived of rights
and stripped of all dignity,
remember that we enter this world
naked and unadorned;
bring us into your presence
clothed only with the works of love and justice
which you have prepared for us,
for you are our Saviour,
now and for ever.
R/. Amen.

The procession moves to the eleventh station, singing the hymn chosen. When all have gathered, a reader announces:

The eleventh station – where Jesus is nailed to the cross.

V/. We adore you, O Christ, and we bless you:
R/. Because by your holy cross you have redeemed the world.

The reader reads Mark 15:25–28.

The response is sung, as above.

Silence is kept; intercession may be offered.

Collect

Christ, victim for our deliverance,
you stretched out your arms
to embrace our broken world;
let us not refuse the love which created and sustains us,
but make us practise it
in care of our neighbour's need,
you whose pierced hands uphold us
now and for ever.
R/. Amen.

The Way of the Cross

The procession moves to the twelfth station, singing the hymn chosen. When all have gathered, a reader announces:

The twelfth station – where Jesus dies on the cross.

V/. We adore you, O Christ, and we bless you:
R/. Because by your holy cross you have redeemed the world.

The reader reads Luke 23:44–49.

The response is sung, as above.

Silence is kept; intercession may be offered.

Collect

Christ, our life,
you emptied yourself of glory
and chose to die as one of us,
enduring the death of a slave.
Into your death we have been baptized,
so let us live in your new and risen life,
inspired and empowered by your Spirit,
now and for ever.
R/. Amen.

The procession moves to the thirteenth station, singing the hymn chosen. When all have gathered, a reader announces:

The thirteenth station – where the body of Jesus is placed in the arms of Mary, his mother.

V/. We adore you, O Christ, and we bless you:
R/. Because by your holy cross you have redeemed the world.

The reader reads Lamentations 2:11–12.

The response is sung, as above.

Silence is kept; intercession may be offered.

The Way of the Cross

Collect

Christ, son of Mary,
you taught that all who mourn are blessed;
comfort those whose grief
is more than they can bear,
and give them strength
to surrender their sorrows into your hands,
for you are the consoler of humankind,
now and for ever.
R/. Amen.

The procession moves to the fourteenth station, singing the hymn chosen. When all have gathered, a reader announces:

The fourteenth station – where Jesus is laid in the tomb.

V/. We adore you, O Christ, and we bless you:
R/. Because by your holy cross you have redeemed the world.

The reader reads John 19:38–42.

The response is sung, as above.

Silence is kept; intercession may be offered.

Collect

Christ, our hope,
you rested in the tomb
on the Sabbath day.
Give us the patience to wait
and the courage to encounter darkness,
knowing that in your risen life
there is the dawn of a new and unending day,
now and for ever.
R/. Amen.

The Way of the Cross

The procession now gathers before the altar, or at the point where it began.

Minister:
Christ, Saviour of the world,
who by your cross and precious blood have redeemed us:

People:
Save us and help us, we pray to you, O Lord.

Minister:
Let us pray.

A short silence is kept.

Collect

Christ, eternal Word,
you shared our human nature
and stood with us in the darkness
of abandonment and death.
We beg you,
flood your Church with the light
of your glorious rising from the dead,
so that without doubt or fear
we may walk in the way of salvation.
For you are our life,
now and for ever.
R/. Amen.

The Way of the Cross: Scriptural Series of Stations

A suitable hymn may be sung to begin the service. The minister and people make the sign of the cross as the minister says:

In the name of the Father, and of the Son, and of the Holy Spirit.
R/. Amen.

The Minister and people recite alternately:

V/. Lord, have mercy:
R/. Lord, have mercy.
V/. Christ, have mercy:
R/. Christ, have mercy.
V/. Lord, have mercy:
R/. Lord, have mercy.

All then recite the Lord's Prayer.

The minister may say:

We gather here
to walk the way of the cross
in union with our Saviour Jesus Christ.

We follow the story of his passion
as it is related to us in the Gospel;
we retrace the steps of the Son of Man
as he is betrayed and put on trial,
condemned and put to death.
We remember his words:
'If any desire to be my disciple,
let them deny themselves,
take up their cross every day
and follow me.'

Let us be still for a moment,
and name the cross that we are carrying.

The Way of the Cross

Let us remember also the many forms of the cross
carried by the poor, the oppressed and the sick,
in union with Christ.

Silent prayer

Collect

God of compassion, look upon your people,
for whose sake your Son Jesus Christ
freely chose to undergo the torment of the cross;
who is alive, in one glory with you and the Holy Spirit,
now and for ever.
R/. Amen.

*The procession moves to the first station, singing the verse(s) of a
hymn. In this second series, verses of the hymn* Stabat Mater
*(New English Hymnal 97) may be sung between each station.
Other hymns may also be used.*

When the people have gathered, a reader says:

The first station on the way of the cross – Gethsemane, where
Jesus prays.

The reader says:
V/. Lord, by your cross and resurrection, you have set us free.
R/. You are the Saviour of the world.

All kneel in silence for a moment.

The reader reads Matthew 26:36–44.

A suitable response is sung. See above, p. 265.

Silence is kept; suitable intercessions may be offered.

The Way of the Cross

Collect

In a garden, O God,
we took our own way
and lost your friendship;
now in this garden,
one who is our flesh and blood
has pledged himself
to take your way, even unto death.
Teach us how to be faithful
as Christ your Son was faithful,
that we may truly be your children.
We ask this in his name.
R/. Amen.

*The procession moves to the second station, singing the verse(s)
of a hymn. When the people have gathered, a reader says:*

The second station on the way of the cross – Gethsemane, where
Jesus is betrayed.

The reader says:
V/. Lord, by your cross and resurrection, you have set us free.
R/. You are the Saviour of the world.

All kneel in silence for a moment.

The reader reads Matthew 26:45–50.

A suitable response is sung.

Silence is kept; intercessions may be offered.

Collect

God of truth,
forgive us when we betray your trust

and lead us back again
to the ways of sincerity,
that our deeds may prove our words,
and our lives be lived with integrity
as disciples of Christ.
We ask this in his name.
R/. Amen.

*The procession moves to the third station, singing the verse(s) of
a hymn. When the people have gathered, a reader says:*

The third station on the way of the cross – the Sanhedrin, where
Jesus is put on trial.

The reader says:
V/. Lord, by your cross and resurrection, you have set us free.
R/. You are the Saviour of the world.

All kneel in silence for a moment.

The reader reads Mark 14:55–64.

A suitable response is sung.

Silence is kept; intercessions may be offered.

Collect

God, whose Son,
though innocent, was tried as guilty,
and found to deserve death;
let all who are unjustly accused
be given the words to answer injustice
with the power of love,
as followers of Christ.
We ask this in his name.
R/. Amen.

*The procession moves to the fourth station, singing the verse(s)
of a hymn. When the people have gathered, a reader says:*

The fourth station on the way of the cross – where Peter denies
Jesus.

The reader says:
V/. Lord, by your cross and resurrection, you have set us free.
R/. You are the Saviour of the world.

All kneel in silence for a moment.

The reader reads Luke 24:50–62.

A suitable response is sung.

Silence is kept; intercessions may be offered.

Collect

God,
whose steadfast love abides;
keep us true to your name,
so that we never deny you,
either by word or deed,
but remain faithful to Christ.
We ask this in his name.
R/. Amen.

*The procession moves to the fifth station, singing the verse(s) of
a hymn. When the people have gathered, a reader says:*

The fifth station on the way of the cross – the Roman
Headquarters, where Pilate judges Jesus.

The reader says:
V/. Lord, by your cross and resurrection, you have set us free.
R/. You are the Saviour of the world.

The Way of the Cross

All kneel in silence for a moment.

The reader reads Mark 15:1–15.

A suitable response is sung.

Silence is kept; intercessions may be offered.

Collect

God, you so loved the world
that you gave your only Son:
the innocent in exchange for the guilty,
the blameless in the place of the sinner.
As Christ has taken his stand with us in being human,
so fashion us after the likeness of your humanity.
We ask this in his name.
R/. Amen.

*The procession moves to the sixth station, singing the verse(s) of
a hymn. When the people have gathered, a reader says:*

The sixth station on the way of the cross – where Jesus is beaten
and crowned with thorns.

The reader says:
V/. Lord, by your cross and resurrection, you have set us free.
R/. You are the Saviour of the world.

All kneel in silence for a moment.

The reader reads Mark 15:15–20.

A suitable response is sung.

Silence is kept; intercessions may be offered.

The Way of the Cross

Collect

God of glory,
you did not hide your Christ
from beatings and ridicule;
steady your people,
and give them patience
when they are called
to suffer injustice
because they are Christ's disciples.
We ask this in his name.
R/. Amen.

*The procession moves to the seventh station, singing the verse(s)
of a hymn. When the people have gathered, a reader says:*

The seventh station on the way of the cross – where Jesus takes
up the cross.

The reader says:
V/. Lord, by your cross and resurrection, you have set us free.
R/. You are the Saviour of the world.

All kneel in silence for a moment.

The reader reads John 19:14–17.

A suitable response is sung.

Silence is kept; intercessions may be offered.

Collect

God, whose purpose it was
that your Christ should carry the cross
to expel from our midst
the power of our ancient enemy;

let the enemy be killed in us
by the power of that same cross,
that we may live
in the light of Christ's resurrection.
We ask this in his name.
R/. Amen.

*The procession moves to the eighth station, singing the verse(s)
of a hymn. When the people have gathered, a reader says:*

The eighth station on the way of the cross – where Simon of
Cyrene carries the cross.

The reader says:
V/. Lord, by your cross and resurrection, you have set us free.
R/. You are the Saviour of the world.

All kneel in silence for a moment.

The reader reads Mark 15:20–21.

A suitable response is sung.

Silence is kept; intercessions may be offered.

Collect

Sustain us, O God;
let us not grow weary
as we follow Christ on the way of the cross,
but support us and keep us faithful,
so that for us his burden may be light
and his yoke easy to bear,
since he is carrying it with us.
We ask this in his name.
R/. Amen.

The procession moves to the ninth station, singing the verse(s) of a hymn. When the people have gathered, a reader says:

The ninth station on the way of the cross – where Jesus meets the women of Jerusalem.

The reader says:
V/. Lord, by your cross and resurrection, you have set us free.
R/. You are the Saviour of the world.

All kneel in silence for a moment.

The reader reads Luke 23:27–31.

A suitable response is sung.

Silence is kept; intercessions may be offered.

Collect

God, our Father,
let this contemplation of Christ's passion
make us compassionate to all who suffer,
so that in care and concern for them
we may give you worship that is genuine
and practise a religion that is true and faultless
as disciples of Jesus.
We ask this in his name.
R/. Amen.

The procession moves to the tenth station, singing the verse(s) of a hymn. When the people have gathered, a reader says:

The tenth station on the way of the cross – Golgotha, where Jesus is crucified.

The reader says:
V/. Lord, by your cross and resurrection, you have set us free.
R/. You are the Saviour of the world.

All kneel in silence for a moment.

The reader reads Matthew 27:33–37.

A suitable response is sung.

Silence is kept; intercessions may be offered.

Collect

God, who in the crucifixion of your Christ
reached out your hands
to embrace all men and women;
let us not refuse
the love which created and sustains us,
but make us practise it
in care of our neighbour's need,
according to Christ's command.
We ask this in his name.
R/. Amen.

*The procession moves to the eleventh station, singing the verse(s)
of a hymn. When the people have gathered, a reader says:*

The eleventh station on the way of the cross – where Jesus
promises Paradise to the thief.

The reader says:
V/. Lord, by your cross and resurrection, you have set us free.
R/. You are the Saviour of the world.

All kneel in silence for a moment.

The reader reads Luke 23:39–43.

A suitable response is sung.

Silence is kept; intercessions may be offered.

Collect

Remember us, O God,
when you look upon the face of Christ,
and as we have nothing to commend us to you,
let your compassion give us everything.
We ask this in his name.
R/. Amen.

*The procession moves to the twelfth station, singing the verse(s)
of a hymn. When the people have gathered, a reader says:*

The twelfth station on the way of the cross – where Mary and
John stand beneath the cross.

The reader says:
V/. Lord, by your cross and resurrection, you have set us free.
R/. You are the Saviour of the world.

All kneel in silence for a moment.

The reader reads John 19:25–27.

A suitable response is sung.

Silence is kept; intercessions may be offered.

Collect

God and Father of all,
as Mary and John were given
into each other's care as mother and son,

let the passion of Christ move us
to care for those who are orphaned and widowed,
that we may truly be the brothers and sisters
of your Son, Jesus Christ.
We ask this in his name.
R/. Amen.

The procession moves to the thirteenth station, singing the verse(s) of a hymn. When the people have gathered, a reader says:

The thirteenth station on the way of the cross – where Jesus dies on the cross.

The reader says:
V/. Lord, by your cross and resurrection, you have set us free.
R/. You are the Saviour of the world.

All kneel in silence for a moment.

The reader reads John 19:28–30.

A suitable response is sung.

Silence is kept; intercessions may be offered.

Collect

Gracious God,
whose Son by dying
accomplished the work
for which you had sent him;
pour out on us the Spirit
that is released by the death of Jesus,
that we may have eternal life in him.
We ask this in his name.
R/. Amen.

The procession moves to the fourteenth station, singing the verse(s) of a hymn. When the people have gathered, a reader says:

The fourteenth station on the way of the cross – the tomb where Jesus is laid.

The reader says:
V/. Lord, by your cross and resurrection, you have set us free.
R/. You are the Saviour of the world.

All kneel in silence for a moment.

The reader reads John 19:38–42.

A suitable response is sung.

Silence is kept; intercessions may be offered.

Collect

God, our life,
from whose love
neither death nor the grave
will separate us;
give us the patience to wait
and the courage to encounter darkness,
knowing that in the resurrection of Jesus
there is the dawn of a new and unending day.
We ask this in his name.
R/. Amen.

The procession moves to the fifteenth station, singing the verse(s) of a hymn. When the people have gathered, a reader says:

In wonder and amazement, we stand before the tomb of Jesus.

The Way of the Cross

The reader says:
V/. Lord, by your cross and resurrection, you have set us free.
R/. You are the Saviour of the world.

All kneel in silence for a moment.

The reader reads John 20:1–10.

A suitable response is sung.

Silence is kept; intercessions may be offered.

Or the minister may say:

Let us praise Christ,
the risen One, the First and the Last.
All reply: Praise to you, Lord Jesus Christ.
or: Kyrie eleison.

Risen Christ,
you have ended the rule of death:
All reply: Praise to you, Lord Jesus Christ.
or: Kyrie eleison.

Risen Christ,
you have left the darkness of the tomb:
All reply: Praise to you, Lord Jesus Christ.
or: Kyrie eleison.

Risen Christ,
you will come again in glory:
All reply: Praise to you, Lord Jesus Christ.
or: Kyrie eleison.

Risen Christ,
you will transform us into your likeness:

All reply: Praise to you, Lord Jesus Christ.
or: Kyrie eleison.

Collect

Gracious God,
listen to your people's prayer,
that having walked with Christ
the way of the cross,
we may walk always with him
in the paths of the gospel.
We ask this in his name.
R/. Amen.

Minister:
Let us bless the Lord.

All:
Thanks be to God.

Minister:
May God bless us,
guard us from all evil
and bring us to eternal life.
R/. Amen.

PART ELEVEN

A LITURGY OF FORGIVENESS

It would be most appropriate to use this service towards the end of Lent or in Holy Week, as a preparation for Easter.

As the congregation gathers, they are invited to mark their fore-heads with ashes, as on Ash Wednesday.

The service begins in silence. The president and other ministers enter and kneel facing the altar. All kneel. Silence is kept. After a while, all stand.

The president may introduce the service with words such as these:

V/. The Lord be with you,
R/. And also with you.

Dear friends in Christ,
day by day throughout the time of Lent
God speaks to our hearts
and with tender love
invites us to turn from sin,
to reject the attractions of evil
and embrace the gospel.

Let us come without fear
and approach with confidence
the place of God's forgiveness,
that our guilt may be wiped away,
and our hearts opened to receive
the reconciliation which is found in Christ.

Let us pray.

Collect

God of patient love,
forgive the wrong that we have done,
so that by your goodness we may be released
from everything that enslaves us
and set free to serve you in peace.
We make this prayer through Jesus Christ,
who is one with you and the Holy Spirit,
now and for ever.

The Ministry of the Word

*Selections may be made from this list of readings. A suitable
responsorial psalm is attached to each of the readings from the
Old Testament and the letters of the New Testament.*

Old Testament Readings

Genesis 3:1–19
Adam and Eve eat the fruit and are judged by God
Psalm 38:1–4, 21, 22

Exodus 20:1–21
The Ten Commandments are given on Mount Sinai
Psalm 19:7–11

2 Samuel 12:1–11, 13
The Prophet Nathan accuses David of adultery
Psalm 51:1–10

Isaiah 1:10–20
The Prophet castigates the sinful nation
Psalm 51:11–18

Isaiah 5:1–7
The Parable of the Vineyard
Psalm 80:9–19

Isaiah 55:1–11
Isaiah speaks of the closeness and compassion of God
Psalm 119:145–152

Joel 2:12–19
A call to repentance and fasting
Psalm 130

Readings from the Letters of the New Testament

Romans 5:6–11
Paul writes of the reconciliation brought by Christ
Psalm 32

Romans 6:2–13
Paul writes of the new birth symbolically enacted in baptism
Psalm 16

Romans 12:1–19
Paul names the gifts necessary for the unity of the Church
Psalm 133

2 Corinthians 5:16–21
Paul writes of the new creation in Christ
Psalm 103:1–10

Galatians 5:16–25
Paul names the fruits of the Spirit
Psalm 85

Ephesians 4:1–5, 17–32
Paul writes of the spiritual revolution that is life in Christ
Psalm 95

Ephesians 5:1–14
Paul invites his listeners to live as children of light
Psalm 112

Colossians 3:1–17
Paul writes of the new life of the resurrection
Psalm 30

1 John 1:5—2:2
John proclaims the fellowship of Christians with the incarnate Christ
Psalm 100

Acclamation: Psalm 51:10

V/. Christ our Saviour, glory to you!
R/. Christ our Saviour, glory to you!
V/. Create in me a clean heart, O God,
and put a new and right spirit within me.
R/. Christ our Saviour, glory to you!

Gospel Readings

Matthew 5:1–12
The Beatitudes

Matthew 5:13–20
Jesus fulfils the Law

Matthew 5:21–30
'You have heard it said . . . but I say . . .'

Matthew 5:33–42
The perfect way

Matthew 5:43–48
Love your enemies

Matthew 6:1–18
Prayer, alms, fasting

Matthew 6:24–34
Seek first the rule of God

Matthew 18:21–35
The king settling accounts with his slaves

Matthew 25:31–46
The sheep and the goats

Luke 15:1–10
Rejoicing in heaven over one repentant sinner

Luke 15:11–32
The two sons

Luke 18:9–14
The Pharisee and the tax collector

Luke 19:1–10
Zacchaeus

John 8:1–11
The adulteress is forgiven

John 15:1–11
Live in Christ and bear fruit

A short address may follow the Gospel.

The Act of Sorrow follows. Two forms are suggested here. The reader should make appropriate pauses and there should be time for reflection.

A Liturgy of Forgiveness

First form of the Act of Sorrow (cf. Matthew 5:1–11)

President: Let us take to heart the blessings of the kingdom of heaven in a spirit of repentance and faith.

Reader: Jesus said: 'Blessed are the poor in spirit, for theirs is the kingdom of heaven.'

             For our overbearing spirit;
for our self-centredness;
for our addiction to possessions:

All: Jesus, have mercy on me, a sinner.

Reader: Jesus said: 'Blessed are the gentle, for they shall inherit the earth.'

             For our anger and bad temper;
for our violence in word and deed;
for the abuse of the earth, our home:

All: Jesus, have mercy on me, a sinner.

Reader: Jesus said: 'Blessed are those who weep, for they shall be comforted.'

             For our lack of compassion;
for our indifference to others' grief;
for all that we mourn in our own life:

All: Jesus, have mercy on me, a sinner.

Reader: Jesus said: 'Blessed are those who hunger and thirst after justice, for they shall be satisfied.'

             For our lack of justice to those around us;
for economic and political injustice and oppression;
for our connivance at the wrong done by others:

A Liturgy of Forgiveness

All: Jesus, have mercy on me, a sinner.

Reader: Jesus said: 'Blessed are those who show mercy, for they shall receive mercy.'

For our intolerance and judgemental spirit;
for the lack of forgiveness we harbour in our hearts;
for our lack of mercy to one another:

All: Jesus, have mercy on me, a sinner.

Reader: Jesus said: 'Blessed are the pure in heart, for they shall see God.'

For all that is crooked in our hearts;
for evil thoughts, lustful feelings and self-indulgence;
for lack of honesty with ourselves and others:

All: Jesus, have mercy on me, a sinner.

Reader: Jesus said: 'Blessed are those who make peace, for they shall be called children of God.'

For quarrels and longstanding bitterness;
for war, bloodshed and mischief;
for the abuse and neglect of the young:

All: Jesus, have mercy on me, a sinner.

Reader: Jesus said: 'Blessed are those who suffer persecution for the sake of justice, for theirs is the kingdom of heaven.'

For intolerance in our hearts and in our world;
for neglect of prayer for the oppressed;
for silence in the face of injustice:

All: Jesus, have mercy on me, a sinner.

A Liturgy of Forgiveness

Second form of the Act of Sorrow

Reader: God says: 'I will pour clean water upon you and you shall be cleansed from all your unfaithfulness. I will give you a new heart and a new spirit. I will write my law upon your heart and you shall know that I am God.'

As a people called to serve the One who alone is Just and Holy,
we acknowledge our unworthiness and failure in service:

All: A new heart, a new spirit, create for me, O God.

Reader: Like Adam and Eve we are called to be stewards of creation;
forgive our misuse of your gifts, our greed and spoiling of the earth.

All: A new heart, a new spirit, create for me, O God.

Reader: Like Abraham and Sarah we are called to put our trust in One we cannot see;
forgive our lack of faith, our desire to serve gods we can see.

All: A new heart, a new spirit, create for me, O God.

Reader: Like Moses, we are called to be prophets of liberation;
forgive our enslavement to comfort, our seeking of self-fulfilment.

All: A new heart, a new spirit, create for me, O God.

Reader: Like Isaiah, we are called to speak God's judgement and consoling love;
forgive our hardness of heart and lack of judgement.

A Liturgy of Forgiveness

All: A new heart, a new spirit, create for me, O God.

Reader: Like John the Baptist, we are called to decrease, so that
Christ may be greater;
forgive our self-importance, our seeking the approval
of our neighbours.

All: A new heart, a new spirit, create for me, O God.

Reader: Like Mary, we are called to be Christ-bearers, open to
God's word;
forgive our deaf ears and lack of faith.

All: A new heart, a new spirit, create for me, O God.

Reader: Like John, we are Christ's beloved brothers and sisters;
forgive our strife with those we love and respect.

All: A new heart, a new spirit, create for me, O God.

Reader: Like the apostles, we are called by Christ to be his witnesses everywhere;
forgive our timidity and trivial preoccupations.

All: A new heart, a new spirit, create for me, O God.

Reader: Like Paul, we are chosen by Christ to display his mercy
in us;
forgive our lack of mercy towards others.

All: A new heart, a new spirit, create for me, O God.

Reader: Christ calls us to love one another, to bear each other's
burdens and so fulfil his law. We ask forgiveness for
failures in community, in faith, in service and in love.

All: A new heart, a new spirit, create for me, O God.

A Liturgy of Forgiveness

After the Act of Sorrow, a silence is kept.

All then recite together this confession:

Father of all, we come before you
seeking your forgiveness and peace.
We have made burdens for ourselves
and forced others to carry them.
We have done wrong ourselves
and connived at wrongs done by others.
We live so close to suffering
yet are slow to bring relief.
Have pity on us, see the tears
wept for ourselves and for this broken world.
Lay your hands upon us
to heal, forgive and reconcile.
By the gentle working of the Holy Spirit
set us free to be faithful to the gospel
and walk in the way of Jesus.
Amen.

*The members of the congregation then come to the president,
who wipes off the ashes from their forehead, then lays a hand on
their head or shoulder and says:*

N. God forgives you. Be at peace.

*The people remain standing around the president. When all have
received the laying on of hands, the president stretches out
her/his hands over them all and says:*

Strong and loving God,
through the death and resurrection of your Christ
you have reconciled all things to yourself
and sent the Holy Spirit
for the forgiveness of sins.
Be present to us who await your love;
touch us with your healing hand.

Grant release from our guilt
and pardon for our offences.
Set us free from the burdens
that oppress our spirit.
Reconcile us to you in peace
and to those about us in mutual charity.
We ask this through Christ, our Lord.
R/. Amen.

or:

God of compassion,
accept the prayer of those
who bow their heads before you
in sorrow for their sins.
Grant them forgiveness
and set them free to walk with joy
in the way of your commandments.
We ask this in the name of Jesus,
our Saviour, now and for ever.
R/. Amen.

The president gives the absolution:

In the name of Christ
who forgives and heals and raises up,
and by the ministry of the Holy Spirit in the Church,
you are absolved from all your sins.

And may the blessing of almighty God,
The Father, the Son and the Holy Spirit,
be with you and remain with you always.
R/. Amen.

*All exchange a sign of peace. A suitable hymn of thanksgiving
may conclude the service.*

PART TWELVE

THE SERVICE OF TENEBRAE

The service known as 'Tenebrae' originated in the Middle Ages. It is a form of the monastic Office of Vigils, originally recited at night, combined with that of Lauds, originally celebrated at dawn. Tenebrae took on a specific and dramatic form when celebrated on Maundy Thursday, Good Friday and Easter Saturday. From the medieval period the whole service was 'anticipated', or held on the evenings before the days in question, beginning on the evening of the Wednesday of Holy Week.

Tenebrae ('The Darkness') acquired its dramatic character by being held in the hours of darkness, as its name implies. Tenebrae begins by candlelight and ends in darkness. It is a stark contrast to the Easter Vigil, which begins in darkness and blazes into light as a symbol of Christ the risen light. As a service that traditionally accompanies the last days of Holy Week, Tenebrae is a dark prelude to the light of Easter, a celebration of Christ's Passion in anticipation of his rising from the dead.

At Tenebrae, the passage from light to darkness is brought about through extinguishing candles at various points throughout the service. Traditionally, fifteen candles mounted upon a large triangular candlestick were extinguished one by one, leaving only a single candle burning. This represented the light of Christ, and was symbolically 'buried' by being hidden behind the altar.

The other dramatic feature of 'Tenebrae' is the chanting of texts from the book of Lamentations, attributed to the Prophet Jeremiah and describing the desolation of Jerusalem after its destruction by Nebuchadnezzar in 586 BCE. In the development of the medieval services, these readings were 'applied' as a dramatic commentary on the betrayal, trial and crucifixion of Jesus. Readings alternate with responses, which take and juxtapose short texts largely from Scripture to meditate on the same themes.

After the Second Vatican Council, the reform of the daily prayer of the Catholic Church abolished Tenebrae. However, its character and the superb music composed for the responsories and Lamentations readings by Renaissance composers have ensured that it has not altogether disappeared.

While it would be too difficult nowadays to celebrate the whole service on three successive nights, some adaptations are sometimes made. What follows in this chapter is one such adaptation, which uses material from Tenebrae to build a meditative service around three themes: the Prayer and Agony of Jesus in Gethsemane, the Trial of Jesus and the Death of Jesus.

These themes may be broadened by choices of readings from non-biblical sources, representing the suffering and death of innocents, and reflecting ways in which the Passion of Jesus finds echoes in the modern world.

This service might best be held on the Wednesday evening of Holy Week, as a preparation for the Three Days of Easter.

A large candlestick holding fifteen candles is required. The service is held as far as possible by candlelight and the congregation should carry candles. The candles on the candlestick are extinguished during the service at the points indicated. At the end, when the reader says 'And it was night', the fourteenth candle is put out. Simultaneously, the congregation blow out their candles. The fifteenth candle is left burning alone in the darkness.

Introduction

It is appropriate for the congregation to be seated during the body of the service, except for the opening prayer, hymns and the concluding Gospel reading, when everyone should stand. If more variety is required, people may kneel or stand during the collects.

The congregation gathers, and all the candles are lit. The leader of the service may say a few words of introduction to the service. The congregation are then invited to stand for the opening prayer.

If it is not possible for the readings from Lamentations to be chanted all the way through, the text may be spoken and the final sentence Jerusalem, Jerusalem . . . *might be sung by the congregation as a response.*

Prayer
Faithful God,
look upon your people,
for whose sake our Saviour Jesus Christ
freely accepted betrayal, rejection
and death upon the Cross;
who now in glory pleads for us,
for ever and ever.
R/. Amen.

Part One: The Prayer and Agony in the Garden

The congregation are invited to sit down. The Taizé response 'Stay with me' is sung and repeated several times.

A reader reads the Gospel, Mark 14:32–42.
The Prayer and Agony of Jesus in Gethsemane

The hymn 'Praise to the Holiest' (New English Hymnal 439) is sung.

Collect

Father,
you have entrusted everything
into your Son's hands,

and he offers himself
that we may be consecrated in the truth.
As we accompany him in vigil,
keep us awake,
save us from the time of trial
and deliver us out of darkness
into the light of his resurrection,
for you have loved us for ever and ever.
R/. Amen.

The first candle is extinguished.

A reader reads Lamentations 1:1–7.

The La-men-ta-tions of the Pro-phet Je - re - mi - ah. Al - eph.

How_ lone-ly she sits, the ci - ty once full of peo- ple, once the great-est

a - mong na-tions, now she is a wid- ow, once queen_ a - mong the

pro - vin- ces, now she is re- duced to sla - ve - ry. Beth.

She weeps bit - ter - ly through the night, tears run down her cheeks,

not_ one of her lov - ers is there to com-fort her, all her friends

have re - ject- ed her and be- come her e - ne- mies. Gi - mel.

Cruel_ is the ex - ile, long the sla - ve - ry where Ju - dah has gone,

scat - tered a - mong the pa - gans with no - where to lay her head;

all her per - se - cu - tors fell up - on her and left her no es - cape.

Da - leth. The roads to Zi - on are de - sert - ed,

no pil - grims at - tend her ho - ly days, her gates are bro - ken down,

her priests in des - pair, her young wo - men clothed in rags, and she

her - self bowed down in bit - ter - ness. He. E - ne - mies now

lord it o - ver her, boast - ing of their tri - umph; the Lord has

con - demned her for her ma - ny, ma - ny sins, her chil - dren dri - ven

in - to cap - ti - vi - ty be - fore their op - pres - sor. Jer - u - sal - em,

Jer - u - sal - em! Turn a - gain! Re - turn to the Lord your God!

Responsory 1

V/. Lament, my people, like a virgin bride:
R/. Shepherds, show your grief in sackcloth and ashes.
V/. Because the day of the Lord approaches, that great and bitter day:
R/. Priests, clothe yourselves in sackcloth.

V/. Ministers of the altar, weep and cover yourselves with dust:
R/. Because the day of the Lord approaches, that great and
bitter day.

The second candle is extinguished.

Psalm 55:1–9, 18–20 is recited.

Refrain (if sung as a responsorial psalm):

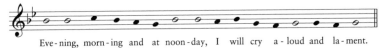

Eve - ning, morn - ing and at noon - day, I will cry a - loud and la - ment.

Tone:

Responsory 2

V/. They have betrayed me into the hands of the wicked:
R/. And thrown me among sinners, giving me no quarter.
V/. The mighty have gathered against me and stood before me
like giants:
R/. Aliens have risen against me, the mighty are bent on my
destruction.
V/. The mighty have gathered against me:
R/. And stood before me like giants.

The third candle is extinguished.

Reading: Jeremiah 20:8–12.
*The Prophet complains before God, but resolves to go on with
his mission.*

Responsory 3

V/. I have been numbered among those condemned to the
grave:
R/. Free among the dead, as one beyond help.

V/. They have laid me in the depths of the grave:
R/. In darkness and in the shadow of death.
V/. I have become as one beyond help:
R/. Free among the dead, among those condemned to the grave.

Collect

You lead us, O Christ,
through dark and desolate places,
for you have entered the abyss
and known the depths of abandonment.
Put hope in our steps
and light on our path,
that we may have words to counsel the despairing
and strength to support the faint hearted;
you who suffered and bore our grief,
our Saviour, now and for ever.
R/. Amen.

The fourth candle is extinguished.

There is a pause for reflection.

Part Two: The Trial of Jesus

*The Hymn 'Ah holy Jesu' (*New English Hymnal *62) is sung, or another suitable song.*

Collect

Christ, our Saviour,
judge of heaven and earth,
you allowed yourself to be put on trial
and condemned at human hands.
Give us courage to live by your justice,
so that we may face your judgement without fear;

308

for you are our redeemer,
now and for ever.
R/. Amen.

The reading from Lamentations is continued (1:10–13).

Jod. The e - ne - my has stretched out hands o - ver

the trea - sures of the ci - ty; she has seen the na - tions in - vade her

sanc - tu - a - ry, those whom you for - bade to en - ter your as - sem - bly.

Caph. In an - guish the peo - ple search for bread, they

trade their trea - sures for food to re - vive their strength; 'Look, O Lord,

and be - hold; for I am des - pised.' Lamed. Is it

noth - ing to you, all you who pass by? Look and see if there is

a - ny sor - row like my sor - row, which the Lord has in - flict - ed

on the day of his burn - ing an - ger. Mem.

In - to my bones he sent fire from on high, spread - ing a net for

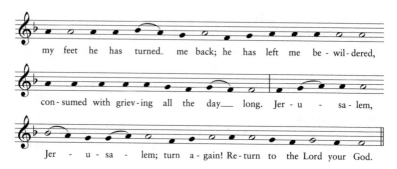

my feet he has turned me back; he has left me be-wil-dered,
con-sumed with griev-ing all the day long. Jer-u - sa-lem,
Jer - u - sa - lem; turn a-gain! Re-turn to the Lord your God.

Responsory 4

V/. We saw him without beauty of majesty, no looks to attract
our eyes:
R/. But he has borne our sins and carried our sorrows.
V/. For our iniquity was he struck down:
R/. We saw him without beauty of majesty.
V/. Truly he has borne our sins and carried our sorrows:
R/. And by his wounds we have been healed.

The fifth candle is extinguished.

Psalm 69:1–3, 8–15 is recited.

Refrain (if sung as a responsorial psalm):

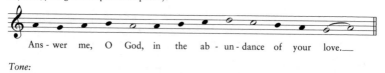

Ans - wer me, O God, in the ab - un - dance of your love.

Tone:

Collect

God, our only hope,
speak to us, lest through weariness
we should not wish to know you;
make us desire to seek your face.

Give us strength to search for you,
even as you have caused us to find you,
and give us the joy
of discovering you more and more.
We ask this through Jesus Christ our Lord.
R/. Amen.

The sixth candle is extinguished.

Old Testament Reading from Wisdom 5:1–10, 15, 16.
The just stand with confidence before their oppressors.

or:

Jeremiah 20:7–13.
The Prophet claims the aid of God as his deliverer.

Responsory 5
V/. My eyes are dim with weeping:
R/. Because I have lost the one who comforted me.
V/. All you who pass this way, look and see:
R/. If there is any sorrow like my sorrow.
V/. For the daughter of my people is smitten:
R/. Struck down with a heavy blow.

The seventh candle is extinguished.

Reading: Jeremiah 14:17–20.
An acknowledgement of guilt, a prayer for God to be faithful

A non-biblical reading might be appropriate here.

Responsory 6

V/. See how the just man dies, and no one cares:
R/. The innocent are taken, and no one sees.
V/. Yet the innocent are now safe from treachery:
R/. And their memorial is one of peace.

V/. Like a lamb in the hands of a shearer:
R/. He was silent, not opening his mouth.
V/. He was captured, judged and taken away:
R/. And his memorial is one of peace.

Collect

God,
around us and in our sight
innocence is trampled,
the guiltless are condemned
and those who have done no wrong
are taken and swallowed up in death.
And when through our tears we ask:
'Where is God?'
show us Christ, your own beloved,
accused, condemned and crucified.
We ask this in his name,
our Saviour, now and for ever.
R/. Amen.

The eighth candle is extinguished.

There is a pause for reflection.

Part Three: The Death of Jesus

*The hymn 'We sing the praise of him who died' (*New English Hymnal *94) is sung, or another suitable song.*

Collect

Infinite God,
before whom darkness is light
and night shines like the day,
show to us, in the night of abandonment,

the light of your faithfulness and love,
and in the depths of despair
come, seek us out and lead us into hope.
We ask this through Jesus Christ.
R/. Amen.

The ninth candle is extinguished.

The reading from Lamentations is resumed (3:1–9).

Al - eph._____ I am one who has seen af - flic - tion be - neath

the rod of God's an - ger. He has dri - ven me and brought me in - to

dark - ness where there is no light; he turns his hand a - gainst me all the

day_ long. Beth._____ He has wast - ed my flesh and my skin,

and bro - ken my bones, he has en - ve - loped me with bit - ter - ness

and be - sieged me with tri - bu - la - tion, he has made me sit in

dark - ness, like the dead long for - got - ten. Gi - mel._____

He has walled me in, I can - not es - cape; though I call and

cry for help, he shuts his ears__ to my prayer; he blocks my ways

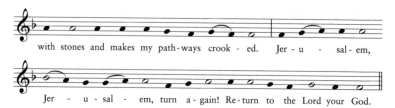

with stones and makes my path-ways crook - ed. Jer - u - sal - em,

Jer - u - sal - em, turn a - gain! Re-turn to the Lord your God.

Responsory 7

V/. Darkness fell when Jesus was crucified,
R/. And at the ninth hour Jesus cried with a loud voice:
V/. My God, my God, why have you forsaken me?
R/. And bowing his head, he breathed his last.
V/. Jesus cried out: Father, into your hands I commend my spirit.
R/. And bowing his head, he breathed his last.

The tenth candle is extinguished.

Psalm 88:1–8, 11–16 is recited.

Refrain (*if sung as a responsorial psalm*):

Lord, let my prayer come be - fore___ you, in - cline your ear to my cry.

Tone:

Collect

Gracious God,
whose Son by dying
accomplished the work
for which you had sent him;
pour out on us the Spirit
that is released by the death of Jesus,

that we may have eternal life in him.
We ask this in his name.
R/. Amen.

The eleventh candle is extinguished.

Reading: Romans 5:1–17.
We have peace with God through Jesus Christ.

Responsory 8

V/. Our Shepherd, the source of living water, has departed.
At his passing the sun was darkened:
R/. He who held the first man captive
has himself been taken captive.
V/. Our Saviour has broken through
the bolts and bars of death:
R/. He has opened the gates of death
and toppled the power of the enemy.
V/. He who held the first man captive
has himself been taken captive:
R/. Our Saviour has broken through
the bolts and bars of death.

The twelfth candle is extinguished.

Reading: Zechariah 12:10–11; 13:7–9.
The prophecy of the scattering of the flock

A non-biblical reading might be appropriate here.

Responsory 9

V/. Christ our life, you were placed in the tomb:
R/. The Angels stood in wonder, beholding your burial.
V/. How can you, who are life, lie in the grave?
R/. By your death you destroyed the power of death.

V/. You are the grain of wheat, sown in the earth:
R/. Which springs up and yields a hundredfold.

The thirteenth candle is extinguished.

The hymn 'Lead, kindly light' (New English Hymnal 392) is sung, or another suitable song.

Collect

Gracious God,
by your gift we come again
to celebrate the days of the life-giving passion
of Christ, your Only-Begotten Son.
Throughout these most holy days,
keep us mindful of this, his Passover mystery,
by which he has saved us and set us free.
We ask this in his name
who is one with you and the Holy Spirit,
now and for ever.
R/. Amen.

The fourteenth candle is extinguished.

A pause for reflection is kept after the Collect.

Then the congregation is invited to stand for the Gospel.

The Gospel is proclaimed:

Gospel Reading: John 13:21–30.
Judas' treachery foretold

On the final phrase of the Gospel: So after receiving the piece of bread, he immediately went out. And it was night. *the congregation blow out their candles, leaving the church lit by the one remaining candle on the candlestick.*

Prayer:
Praise to you, Lord Jesus Christ,
for all the benefits you have given us,
for the pains and insults you have suffered for us.
Merciful Redeemer, friend and brother,
may we know you more clearly,
love you more dearly
and follow you more nearly,
all our days.
R/. Amen.

The Taizé responses 'Within our darkest night' or 'Your word, O Lord, is my light' or 'Our darkness is never dark' may be sung as the congregation departs.

PART THIRTEEN

OTHER MATERIAL FOR THE MAIN SERVICE OF SUNDAY

The Commemoration of Baptism

If the church has a prominent baptismal font near the main doors or on the main axis of the church, it should have a vessel of water placed within or alongside it and the congregation might be asked to turn to face it. Alternatively, a vessel of water might be prepared in the sanctuary or in the centre of the church.

When the ministers have entered, the president greets the people in the usual way and then says this Invitation to Prayer:

Dear friends in Christ,
this is the day
when Jesus passed through the deep waters of death
to risen life in the Holy Spirit.
Let us ask God to renew that same Spirit in us,
that we may live more intensely
the covenant with God which was made in our baptism.

After a brief period of silent prayer, the president recites the following prayer:

Blessed are you, God of all creation,
for water, which cleanses and refreshes the earth;
blessed are you
for the water of life, sprung from the side of Christ
which poured over us your gift of the Spirit
to unite us as members of Christ.

On this day which Christ has made holy
by rising from death,
touch us with this water,
and lead us to him
who is the living spring,
Christ Jesus your beloved,
who lives for ever and ever.

The president sprinkles the people with water.

(A conventional sprinkler might be used, or better, a bunch of rosemary, or sprigs of box, tied together to form a brush.)

During the sprinkling, a psalm or hymn may be sung, for instance:

*Water of Life (*Laudate *512)*
*Baptized in water (*Hymns for Today's Church *381)*

After the sprinkling, Glory to God in the Highest *is sung. The ministers go in procession to the sanctuary if the sprinkling has been done from elsewhere in the church. The Collect follows, and the Ministry of the Word as usual.*

Tropes for the Kyrie

In the first volume of this collection, it was suggested that the acclamation Kyrie eleison *might be amplified by other texts addressed to Christ, known as 'tropes'. The texts are mostly drawn from Scripture and may reflect seasonal needs.*

For Lent

You came to reconcile us to each other and to the Father: Kyrie eleison.
You heal the wounds of our sin and division: Christe eleison.
You intercede for us with the Father: Kyrie eleison.

Christ, healer of the sick:
Jesus, bearer of our sins:
Christ, source of our life:

You bid us be reconciled before we come to your altar:
On the cross you asked forgiveness for sinners:
You give to your Church the ministry of reconciliation:

You make us a new creation by water and the Spirit:
You send your Spirit to create in us a new heart:
You invite us to share in your body and blood:

You gather us to listen to your word:
You open our lips in your praise:
You open our eyes and hearts to others' need:

You desire to lead us from death into life:
You were lifted up to draw all people to yourself:
You shouldered the cross, bearing our suffering and sin:

For Easter, Ascension and Pentecost

Christ, our Passover:
Jesus, our peace:
Christ, our life:

You are the High Priest of the new Covenant:
You build us as living stones in the temple of God:
You make us fellow citizens with your saints:

You have revealed yourself as the way to the Father:
You have poured upon us the Spirit of truth:
You are the Shepherd of eternal life:

You have ascended to God's right hand:
You pour on us the gifts of the Spirit:
You sustain us with the power of your word:

Christ, Alpha and Omega:
Jesus, firstborn from death:
Christ, Lord of all ages:

Anthems at the Fraction

The Litany Agnus Dei – *'Jesus, Lamb of God . . .' – is traditionally sung at the breaking of the eucharistic bread. If real bread is
used and the breaking is prolonged, other anthems may be
appropriate.*

For Lent

(cf. Matthew 4:4; Psalm 33:6; Matthew 8:8)
V/. No one shall live on bread alone:
R/. The word of God is life for all.
V/. By the word of God were the heavens made:
R/. The word of God is life for all.
V/. Speak the word, Lord, and we shall be healed:
R/. The word of God is life for all.

(cf. Psalm 42:3; Psalm 43:3, 4; John 6:34)
V/. My tears have become my bread:
R/. Feed me, O God, with the living bread.
V/. Send forth your light and your faithful love:
R/. Feed me, O God, with the living bread.
V/. And I shall come to the altar of God:
R/. Feed me, O God, with the living bread.

(cf. Revelation 19:7; Psalm 81:16)
V/. This is the bread God gives to feed us:
R/. Let us rejoice and exult and give glory to God.
V/. With the finest wheat, God fed the people:
R/. Let us rejoice and exult and give glory to God.
V/. The marriage feast of the Lamb has come:
R/. Let us rejoice and exult and give glory to God.

Other Material

For Eastertide

(cf. 1 Corinthians 5:7; Romans 6:9)
V/. Christ our Passover is sacrificed for us:
R/. Therefore let us keep the feast.
V/. Christ being raised from the dead will die no more:
R/. Therefore let us keep the feast.
V/. In that he died, he died once for all to sin:
R/. Therefore let us keep the feast.
V/. In that he now lives, he lives to God:
R/. Therefore let us keep the feast.

(cf. Luke 24:13–35; Matthew 28:20)
V/. The disciples knew the Lord in the breaking of the bread:
R/. Abide with us, Lord Jesus Christ!
V/. The risen One unfolded the scriptures to them:
R/. Abide with us, Lord Jesus Christ!
V/. Their eyes were opened and they recognized him:
R/. Abide with us, Lord Jesus Christ!
V/. Jesus said: 'I am with you always, to the end of the age.'
R/. Abide with us, Lord Jesus Christ!

(cf. John 6:48, 50, 58; Psalm 34:8)
V/. I am the living bread, which came down from heaven:
R/. Taste and see that the Lord is good.
V/. I am the true vine, my blood is the true drink:
R/. Taste and see that the Lord is good.
V/. Those who eat and drink of me will have life from me:
R/. Taste and see that the Lord is good.
V/. Anyone who eats this bread will live for ever:
R/. Taste and see that the Lord is good.

PART FOURTEEN

A EUCHARISTIC PRAYER

The idea of having acclamations in the Eucharistic Prayer after the *Sanctus* has in recent years become a feature of prayers in the Roman Catholic Church and the *Common Worship* tradition. Where these acclamations are used, the question is often raised as to their appropriateness. Sometimes critics have suggested that they are merely ornamental and not essential to the prayer.

The acclamations contained in the body of this Eucharistic Prayer are integral to the sense and dynamic of the Eucharist. In the opening section and again in the section beginning 'God most high, look upon this Eucharist . . .', it is the people together with the speaker who make the *epiklesis* – the plea that the Holy Spirit come and fulfil the role announced in the preceding words. Again, during the narrative of the Last Supper, the people make the 'Amen' which, as is the case at the reception of Communion, expresses their desire to become engaged in the movement of Christ's self-offering. The 'Amen' at this point also echoes the traditional Anglican practice of responding 'Amen' at the end of the Prayer of Consecration in the Communion Service according to the *Book of Common Prayer*.

One of the prefaces given in this book is used to begin this prayer.

After the Acclamation Holy, Holy, Holy Lord *the president continues:*

You, God, are the holy One;
source of all being, worthy of all praise.
Blessed is Jesus the Christ
through whom you have given us

the fullness of worship;
for he has offered his body and blood
as the eternal sacrifice,
the gift made present here for us
by the working of the Holy Spirit.

R/. **Amen. Come, Holy Spirit.**

The president continues:

When the hour had come
for Christ freely to give himself up,
he took bread and said the blessing,
broke the bread and gave it to his disciples, saying:
'Take, eat; this is my body which is given for you.
Do this for the remembrance of me.'

R/. **Amen.**

In the same way, after supper,
he took the cup of wine and gave you thanks,
gave the cup to his disciples and said:
'Drink this, all of you;
this is my blood of the new covenant,
which is shed for you and for many
for the forgiveness of sins.
Do this, as often as you drink it,
for the remembrance of me.'

R/. **Amen.**

Mindful of this command, O God,
we hold in remembrance the saving work of Christ:
the death which has destroyed our death,
the rising that promises the glory of all flesh,
the return that will bring your justice
for the living and the dead.

A Eucharistic Prayer

To you we give thanks,
God above all, through all and in all,
and thus we bring before you
the one, holy and living sacrifice.

V/. Great is the mystery of faith:
R/. **Christ has died . . .**

God most high, look upon this Eucharist
sanctified by the Holy Spirit,
and sanctify us who receive these gifts;
unite us in the one living bread
as partakers in the body of Christ,
and through the one cup of his blood
let us taste communion in the Holy Spirit
and the joy of the age to come.

R/. **Amen. Come, Holy Spirit.**

Gracious God, renew the life of your Church:
remember N. our Bishop and all ministers
who break and share the living bread among us.

R/. **Lord, remember.**

Remember those broken in body or spirit:
give them peace in the glorious wounds
by which we have been healed.

R/. **Lord, remember.**

Remember us all, both living and departed;
remember our communion with (Saint N. and all) your saints;
gather your Church together in Christ,
in whom all things in heaven and on earth
are blessed, and made holy,
and raised up before your face eternally.

A Eucharistic Prayer

Through Christ, and with Christ, and in Christ,
in the unity of the Holy Spirit,
all honour and glory is yours,
almighty God and Father,
both now and for ever:

R/. **Amen.**

SOURCES AND
ACKNOWLEDGEMENTS

The texts contained in this book come from several sources. All those who have kindly consented to their material being included are acknowledged below. In some cases material has been modified to suit the context or purpose of the text, for which I offer my thanks.

However, the process of creating texts for worship is complex and any writer will unconsciously find that they have used sources stored in their head, whose exact origin is long forgotten. I am greatly indebted to the tradition of worship, both Anglican and Roman Catholic, in which I have been brought up. Over many years I must have absorbed phrases and images that I cannot now attribute. So should any reader recognize here words, phrases, expressions or patterns of speech that are their own, I would hope that they would understand the difficulty of seeking permission to reproduce what is unconsciously quoted, and also the fact that such unconscious borrowing is a tribute to their work.

If any copyright material is found here which has been used without permission or acknowledgment, this is solely due to my own inadvertence. I or the publishers will be grateful to be informed. The necessary attribution will be included in any future editions.

The Scripture-related opening prayers are original compositions. Many of the other prayers, including the prefaces, are translations or adaptations of texts in the *Missale Romanum* and

Sources and Acknowledgements

Missale Ambrosianum the Roman and Ambrosian (Milanese) missals. Where I have used prefaces from the *Missale Ambrosianum*, these are taken from the versons published in *We Give You Thanks And Praise – The Ambrosian Eucharistic Prefaces* (Canterbury Press, 1999)

All Gospel Acclamations are taken from *The New Revised Standard Version of the Bible* (Anglicized Edition) © 1989, 1995 by the Division of the National Council of Churches of Christ in the United States of America and are used by permission. All rights reserved.

The sourced prayers are taken by permission from the sources listed below. An asterisk indicates that some changes have been made to the text.

The Opening Prayer, Prayer at the Intercession and Prayer after Communion for the feast of Saint David are taken from the National Supplement to the Roman Missal and included by permission of The Roman Catholic Bishops' Conference of England and Wales.

The Alternative form for the *Exsultet* in the Easter Vigil Liturgy was composed by Nathan Mitchell of the Notre Dame Center for Pastoral Liturgy. It is reproduced here by his kind permission.

The Opening Prayer for the Annunciation
The Opening Prayer for Ash Wednesday
The Alternative Opening Prayer for the Second Sunday of Easter
The Opening Prayer for Easter Eve
The Alternative Opening Prayer for Pentecost
are all taken from *All Desires Known* by Janet Morley (MOW 1988, © Janet Morley) and used by kind permission of the SPCK.

The Alternative Opening Prayer for Easter Sunday is excerpted from *The Roman Missal* © 1973, International Commission For English in the Liturgy, Inc. (ICEL); all rights reserved.

The prayers to conclude the Service of Incense for Lent Sundays,* Easter Sundays and Pentecost Eve* in Part 7 Texts for Evening Prayer of Saturday or a Sunday Vigil Service, together with the Prayer of the Service of Light and the Prayer to conclude the Service of Incense from Part 8, Vigils of Ascension Day and Pentecost, are taken from *Proclaiming All Your Wonders, Prayers For A Pilgrim People,* Dominican Publications, Dublin, 1991 and used by permission.

Details of other books cited in the text are:

Come All You People, Shorter Songs for Worship, by John L. Bell and the Wild Goose Worship Group, Wild Goose Publications, Glasgow, 1994

Chants De Taizé 2002–2003, Ateliers et Presses De Taizé, 71250 Taizé Communauté, France. (Collections of Taizé chants also exist in many English publications)

Enemy of Apathy, by John Bell and Graham Maule with the Wild Goose Worship Group, Iona Community 1988

Gather, Comprehensive, GIA Publications, Inc., 7404 South Mason Avenue Chicago, Ill. 60638, 3rd edn, 1986

Hymns For Today's Church, Hodder and Stoughton 1982

Laudate, a Hymn Book for the Liturgy, Decani Music, Mildenhall 1999

Love From Below, by John L. Bell and Graham Maule, Iona Community, Wild Goose Publs., Glasgow, 1989

Songs for the Church's Year, Music for the Feasts and Seasons, by Dom Alan Rees, Rattlesden, Suffolk, Kevin Mayhew, 1995

The New English Hymnal, Canterbury Press, Norwich, 1986

Worship – A Hymnal and Service Book for Roman Catholics, GIA Publications, Inc., Chicago, Ill. 60638, 1994